THE

From the Edge of the World

The Jewish Refugee Experience through Letters and Stories

From the Edge of the World

the World

The Jewish Refugee Experience through Letters and Stories

ANNE JOSEPH

VALLENTINE MITCHELL
LONDON • PORTLAND, OR

First published in 2003 in Great Britain by
VALLENTINE MITCHELL
Crown House, 47 Chase Side, Southgate
London N14 5BP

and in the United States of America by
VALLENTINE MITCHELL
c/o ISBS, 920 NE 58th Avenue, Suite 3000
Portland, OR, 97213-3786

Website: www.vmbooks.com

British Library Cataloguing in Publication Data

From the edge of the world: the Jewish refugee experience
    through letters and stories. – (The library of Holocaust
    testimonies)
    1. Refugees, Jewish – Great Britain – History – 20th century
    2. Refugees, Jewish – Great Britain – Correspondence
    3. Holocaust victims – Correspondence 4. Holocaust, Jewish
    (1939–1945) – Personal narratives 5. Great Britain –
    Emigration and immigration – History – 20th century
    940.5'318142'092241

ISBN 0-85303-472-9 (paper)
ISSN 1363-3759

Library of Congress Cataloging-in-Publication Data

From the edge of the world: the Jewish refugee experience through
letters and stories / edited by Anne Joseph.
    p. cm. – (The library of Holocaust testimonies.)
    ISBN 0-85303-472-9 (pbk.)
    1. Holocaust, Jewish (1939–1945) – Personal narratives.
    2. Refugees, Jewish – England – Correspondence. 3. Holocaust
    survivors – England – Correspondence. 4. Jews – England –
    Correspondence. I. Rockman, Chaim. II. Joseph, Anne, 1935–
    III. Series.

    D804.3.F758 2003
    940.53'18'092241 – dc21
    [B]   2003057159

Typeset in 11/12.25 Palatino by Frank Cass Publishers Ltd
Printed in Great Britain by MPG Books Ltd, Victoria Square, Bodmin, Cornwall

Contents

For Jake and Noah

Acknowledgements

Firstly I would like to thank the following contributors, who allowed me to tamper with their material: Dr Lily Wagner, Irene Kirstein Watts, Lotte Munz, Chaim Bermant, Andrew Herskovits and Rose Ellis. Also to the Wiener Library.

The letters in Part 1 are produced and edited with kind permission from Chaim Rockman. My grateful thanks goes to him for allowing me to dissect his family's letters, and for his infinite patience and advice when I pestered him with innumerable points of clarification.

I would also like to thank Judy Bermant for her recommendations and Michala Barham for her help with layout. Jonny Zucker and Fiona Starr for their ongoing advice and assistance, even when it was not so easy to give, and my mother whose help with German grammar was invaluable, as was her encouragement from afar.

And lastly, but far from least, my thanks to James for his continuous guidance and support and for never allowing me to give up.

Glossary

Note: G = German; H = Hebrew; Y = Yiddish.

chaluz/im (H)	pioneer/s
ganif/ganovim (Y)	thief/thieves
goy/im	non-Jew/s
heimisher (Y)	homely
Hochdeutsch (G)	High German
Judenrein (G)	free of Jews (lit. 'cleansed of' Jews)
kehilla (H)	community
koyach (Y)	strength
mazel (Y)	luck
Mischlinge (G)	person of mixed descent
milchoma (Y)	war
mischpocha (Y)	family
Moshiach (Hebrew)	Messiah
naches (Y)	joy or pride
Pesach (H)	Passover
potz	penis
Rassenschande (G)	Nazi term for a person who was a digrace to their race
Schweinhundt (G)	filthy pig (lit. 'pig-dog')
Shabbes (Y)	Sabbath
Tsores (Y)	troubles
shande (Y)	shameful
shidduch (Y)	a love-match
shmata (Y)	cloth
shocher (Y)	merchant
Staatenlos (G)	stateless
Untermensch (G)	subhuman
varmischt (Y)	confused
Yekke (G)	(lit. jacket): derogatory term for German Jew
Yishuv (H)	settlement/s prior to the establishment of the State of Israel
zezkey (Y):	tart

The Library of Holocaust Testimonies

It is greatly to the credit of Frank Cass that this series of survivors' testimonies is being published in Britain. The need for such a series has been long apparent here, where many survivors made their homes.

Since the end of the war in 1945, the terrible events of the Nazi destruction of European Jewry have cast a pall over our time. Six million Jews were murdered within a short period; the few survivors have had to carry in their memories whatever remains of the knowledge of Jewish life in more than a dozen countries, in several thousand towns, in tens of thousands of villages, and in innumerable families. The precious gift of recollection has been the sole memorial for millions of people whose lives were suddenly and brutally cut off.

For many years, individual survivors have published their testimonies. But many more have been reluctant to do so, often because they could not believe that they would find a publisher for their efforts.

In my own work over the past two decades I have been approached by many survivors who had set down their memories in writing, but who did not know how to have them published. I also realized, as I read many dozens of such accounts, how important each account was, in its own way, in recounting aspects of the story that had not been told before, and adding to our understanding of the wide range of human suffering, struggle and aspiration.

With so many people and so many places involved, including many hundreds of camps, it was inevitable that the historians and students of the Holocaust should find it difficult at times to grasp the scale and range of events. The publication of memoirs is therefore an indispensable part of the extension of knowledge, and of public awareness of the crimes that had been committed against a whole people.

Sir Martin Gilbert
Merton College, Oxford

Foreword

I keep reading that we are in danger of not only 'compassion fatigue' but also (heaven help us) 'Holocaust fatigue'. And it can sometimes be difficult to retain a fresh, open-minded response to the veritable cascade of recent books, films, television programmes and exhibitions about Hitler, Nazism and the horrors and triumphs of World War II.

But I very much hope Anne Joseph's *From the Edge of the World* reaches the widest possible readership. It is a book for our own troubled times – and for several interrelated reasons. In the first place, our world, in the aftermath of '9/11', feels once more under threat. The murderous attacks on iconic buildings in New York and Washington, and subsequently on centres of Western activity and enterprise around the globe, have again forced us to try and confront forces as destructive in their avowed intent as Nazism. Second, the nature of Jewishness is once again being urgently questioned, re-examined, re-defined, in both Israel and the Diaspora – partly in response to a resurgence of virulent anti-Semitism. And, thirdly, new waves of migrants are seeking asylum, in Britain and elsewhere, fleeing oppressive regimes – and anxious about the kind of reception they will receive from ambivalent governments and an often frankly xenophobic press and public.

The analogies between the 1930s and today are far from precise. But, as you read Anne Joseph's moving anthology of letters and stories, by some who escaped from Nazism and others who were consumed by it, it is impossible not to sense powerful resonances for our own times. You may smile at the touching fantasies of some of the 'Hitler Emigres' who made it to Britain (the weekly visit to the cinema felt to one like having a 'box at the opera'), or at the official advice they were given ('DO be as quiet and modest as possible ...'). And you will weep at the final letter from a mother in Leipzig begging her daughter, in vain, to find a way of saving her before she is transported east. Such documents, moving in themselves, also contain important lessons for today. For it is only by understanding the past that we can hope to deal wisely with an insecure present and uncertain future.

Daniel Snowman
2003
(author of *The Hitler Emigres: The Cultural Impact on Britain of Refugees from Nazism*)

Introduction

The idea for this book evolved from two quite separate and yet intrinsically connected events.

The first took place in 1999 when I was doing a charity walk in Israel. During the week I became friendly with Chaim Rockman, the Israeli guide for the group. During a conversation with him he described letters that members of his family had written from Germany, Romania and Britain during the late 1930s/40s. I asked if I could look at them. When I read them I was totally drawn into their tales. In some way they reminded me of stories that my grandmother had told me about her experiences in Germany and then as an immigrant to Britain in the 1930s: stories that she later wrote about.

I had been particularly close to my grandmother; she used to show me her stories once she had finished them, and as a child I had derived enormous pleasure from them. What fascinated and inspired me about my grandmother was the way in which she and my grandfather had adapted to setting up home in a strange country after the trauma of leaving Nazi Germany. I had always been interested in that particular period of their lives. Many years after my grandmother's death, I had deposited some of her stories in Wiener Library in London.

The link was intriguing but I didn't pursue the matter any further at that time.

Then a couple of years ago the painter Polly Rockberger contacted my mother. Polly had been researching her own family background for a series of paintings. During her investigations, she had come across a story written by my grandmother. It was one of the stories that I had given to the Wiener Library. The story had inspired one of Polly's paintings, *Lotte's Apartment*, and she wanted to know if my mother was interested in seeing the painting.

When my mother told me this, the idea for the collection was born. Neither piece was written by professional authors, but in their different ways they managed to describe that particular period in a unique and highly personal way.

I revisited the Wiener Library seeking out other examples of written material by Jewish refugees. I was aware of the huge volume of holocaust survivor testimony that existed, but I was looking for stories that would depict their world as seen through their eyes; describing either the life that they had left or impressions of the one that they had come to. I advertised in several journals and newspapers in order to collect material. The response was fascinating.

As the book developed, it naturally fell two parts. Part 1 is loosely centred on the relatives of those who remained in Nazi Germany and could not get out; while Part 2 comprises those people's stories who did manage to get out. Part 3 reproduces pamphlets from the Central Office for Refugees. It is worth remembering that while they may raise a smile now, at the time, these pamphlets were written (and doubtless taken) very seriously indeed.

The title of this book is a quote taken from one of the letters. Polly's picture is on the front cover of the book. The original is in my home.

Anne Joseph
2002

Part 1
LETTERS

Foreword to Letters

I emigrated to Israel from Manchester with my parents and sister in 1950, at the age of five. At that time we all felt that we were participating in the building of a new society in a new country; the Second World War and the Holocaust were taboo subjects that were not brought up or discussed. As a result of this rather hostile environment concerning anything that was to do with the near-past, we grew up knowing little of my father's history; all we knew was that he had come from Leipzig to England before the war. I had no knowledge of when my father had moved to England, or that the name by which I knew him, Peter, was not his proper name. Nor did I know that he had had a sister who had lived in Romania, or the circumstances of his mother's death. When my father died in 1964, he took all this information with him.

In 1990, when the world was gripped by events in the Persian Gulf, and my family and I were wearing gas-masks sitting in a bomb shelter, I received a telephone call from my sister. She told me things that would eventually open a window to our family's history that I had never known about or suspected. Due to the threat of scud missiles from Iraq she had rearranged her family's bomb shelter, and in doing so she had stumbled across a box of letters that had been sent to my father during the years he had lived in England, 1939–49. Most of the letters were written in German, some in Yiddish and the rest in English. Reading them was a difficult task as the paper was old and had a tendency to crumble in my hand. Many of the letters were written in pencil, which made them difficult to read, and were on all sorts of different materials such as cardboard, wallpaper, the backs of pamphlets, or old stationery.

It was the letters from my grandmother, Lina Rochman, who was trapped in Leipzig with no means of getting out, that left the most dramatic impression on me. These desperate letters were sent to her son Adolf, in Manchester. The letters, written both in broken Yiddish and in phonetic German, are often on scraps of paper which she found in the garbage dump where she worked. The 'paper' on which she wrotes is used to its fullest – the centre of the 'page' as well as around the edges, which made it difficult to know where the letter started and where it ended. She always wrote with a blunt pencil; she had never learned to write with a fountain-pen. What we see so clearly is how her emotional and physical state deteriorates from one letter to another. What is also so striking is the simplicity in which they are written. At the time letters sent via the Red Cross often went back and forth – the sender's letters often returned to the recipient, which is how I managed to own some of the letters that my father had written to his mother and sister.

Through these letters, which are written with much affection, openness and sometimes even with humour, we can gain an understanding of how historical events of the time shaped the lives of ordinary people struggling to survive in extraordinary circumstances.

Chaim Rockman
2002

Oberman–Schmulewitsch Family Tree

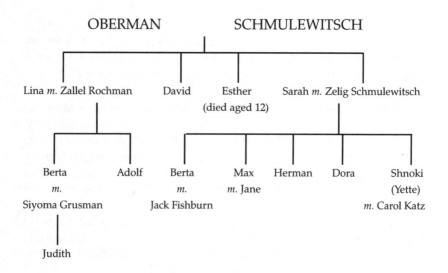

4

Letters

Adolf Rochman was arrested during Kristallnacht in November 1938 and sent for a few weeks to the Oranienburg centre. He was one of the 3,500 stateless (*staatenlos*) Jews who had not managed to leave Leipzig after the deportation of the Polish Jews in October 1938. Whilst he was away his mother, Lina Rochman, had remained in Leipzig. It was at this time that it became clear to them that they needed to leave Germany, and imminently. They had two options: to join Adolf's sister, Berta Grusman, in a small town called Cetata Alba in Romania; or to go to Guisborough in Yorkshire, England, where Adolf's uncle Zelig Schmulewitsch and family had settled a few years earlier, having opened a textile factory. Extracts from the letters begin at this time.

The first letter is from Berta in Romania, to her mother, Lina, and brother, Adolf.

Berta Grusman
Cetata Alba
Saturday, 12 November 1938

Dear Mama and Adolf,
The news about the pogrom reached us today. A *goy* [non-Jew] in town who owns a wireless heard about it first; he immediately went to tell the Rabbi, and then he came to tell us. I was shocked in a way that I've never been before. He said that hundreds of Jewish businesses had been broken into. Hooligans had broken glass from shop windows which they then scattered onto the street so that it looked as if there were crystals on the ground. He also said that all the synagogues had been burned down.

Siyoma's[1] family were also shocked; they always held the Germans to be such cultured people. They can't accept that

---

1. Siyoma was Berta's husband. He held strong communist views.

civilized people, who've given the world 'the best possible musicians, writers, scientists and technology, could do a thing like this. One would expect this sort of pogrom from the Ukrainians, the Poles or the Russians, but not from the Germans.' I wish I had more details, but we're kept in the dark and so all we know is from rumours. Did they burn down Bauburger & Hertz, the big departmental store on the corner of Goethe and Grimmaische Strasse? What happened to the Brodi synagogue in Keil Strasse – was it burned down like all the others? I was told that they didn't touch synagogues that were next door to an Aryan shop or house. They say that they arrested all the Jewish men. Is that true?

I hope that they didn't arrest Adolf – they must know that he can't last long without a proper diet and his insulin. They must know about his diabetes, or I hope he told them if they came to get him. Who would have thought a thing like this could happen in Leipzig of all places? But I must say that I did see it coming, although not in such an extreme way. When the Polish Jews were thrown out in October, one or two families came here, to Cetata Alba. They told us terrible stories of the treatment that they'd got from the German soldiers – as if they were cattle. I can tell you one thing: something like that can never happen here, because they like and respect us. I think, Mama, that the best thing is if you pack up the house and come and live with us. Then you can live in comfort and safety for the rest of your life (you too Adolf).

Judith has a new friend, Larissa, the one whose mother is my seamstress. It's difficult to keep them apart. They are together all the time, in school and after school, during music lessons and horse-riding. At least two nights a week Larissa sleeps here, and sometimes Judith goes to sleep there. Do you remember the photo with Judith dressed up as a marquis? If you still have the picture, you'll see Larissa is on the other side, by the door. She's also dressed as a marquis. All that was for a play they did in school.

When Larissa stays with us I always give them a piano lesson and try to teach them some songs from the Old Country; the ones that Papa used to sing to us. Her mother, I told you, comes from Odessa, which is no more than an hour's train ride from here. She often tells me about it with a lot of nostalgia. She says that Odessa is like Paris with its big wide streets and boulevards which are named after famous French generals and leaders who built the city in the last century. She described Dirbasky Avenue which ends with one of the biggest opera houses in Europe ... What I would give to go and visit, even just once! It's so close, but so far. Now that it's in the hands of the Bolsheviks, who knows what they've done to it? They won't let anyone from a civilized country come and visit.

I must end here, as I have to go and settle some squabbling among the Ukrainian and the Romanian servants.

Write as soon as you can. Think seriously about my suggestion of coming here.

Love to all,
Berta

Among the letters were a few written by Adolf's friends from Leipzig: Hans and Arnold. They had all been participants in the Maccabi swimming team in Leipzig, and both men had stayed illegally in Palestine after the Maccabi Games in 1935.

Nahariya
Tuesday, 15 November 1938

Dear Adolf,
It's been a long time since I last heard from you. I know that it's you who owes me a letter, but I also know what a bad writer you are, so I've taken the initiative to write. What brought pencil to paper this time was the news coming from home. I heard from my parents about the pogrom, already known as Kristallnacht. I'm so thankful that I received a certificate for my parents and brother from the High Commissioner to Palestine in Jerusalem, so that they'll soon be able to leave Leipzig. Like most Jews they had to give up their shares in 'Kaufhaus Joske'.[2] (I remember that you worked for them for some time, just before I left.)

I think that the combination of giving up the business and the pogrom last week was the straw that broke the camel's back, as far as my father was concerned. Remember what a radical supporter he was of the German people and nation! Always walking around with his medals from the Great War, as if the whole of the German army at the time was on his shoulders, saying, 'We the German people will

---

2.   A department store in Leipzig.

7

not let this thug from Austria take over our country.' He, like all the others, is now walking with his tail between his legs. I'm just glad that he and my mother have somewhere else to run to. Just think what could have happened if I hadn't stayed in Palestine after the Maccabi Games in 1935, and had given in to his repeated demands to come back to help in the business, which by that time was already not his.

As you see from the address, we live in Palestine in this small village called Nahariya. Most of its residents (some 300 families) come from all over Germany, and we all work in chicken-farming – something I've never done before, but I quite like it. We're by the sea, so I can go swimming nearly every day, even in what they call winter here, which is warmer than our summers at home. I wouldn't call it fun being under British rule, but it's definitely better and more pleasant than being under the boots of those Brown Shirts.

They call us *Yekkes* [lit. 'jackets'] here which is a degrading name for German Jews. Although being called that is better than being called a 'dirty Jew', it does make me think about who we are. It's ironic, but our relations with the German *goyim* [non-Jews], known as 'Templars', who live in Haifa, is better than with the Polish and Russian Jews.

We don't have much in the way of comfort, as we had back home. Most of us are still living in tents. To go and see a film or a concert we have to go to Beirut or Haifa. But from what I hear about Leipzig, bad as it is here, it's better than being there.

I know you were never a big Zionist, but why don't you try and come and live here with us in the village. Land is cheap (we only had to pay £1000 for four hectares of land plus livestock), the weather is wonderful and you would still be living in a German environment.

Adolf, you must get out while you still have the opportunity, because by the end they will throw all the stateless Jews out to the East, as they did the Polish Jews in October.

I hope to hear from you soon.

Your swimming mate,
Hans

PS. I have found a hectare of land, by the sea. I'm keeping it for you for whenever you come.

The following letter is from Adolf to his Aunt Sarah and Uncle Zelig Schmulewitsch, who had settled in Guisborough, York-shire, and who had a textile factory there.

Humboldtstrasse 3
Leipzig
29 November 1938

Dear Uncle and Aunt,

I hope all is well with you and all my cousins. I'm sorry that we didn't answer your last letter, but I've just come home from the most horrible experience that I've ever known. But first I'd like to congratulate you on your tremendous success. I was so happy and proud that you, together with Max, Herman, Jack and Berta, have managed to build such a big and prosperous business in such a short time. Your factory business letterhead is impressive with your name at the side. I also saw that you have outlets in Glasgow and Manchester.

How's Aunt Sarah managing in the new country? Can she already speak the language? Is there a theatre in Newcastle, as I know that she likes to go from time to time? I saw on the map that it's no more than ten kilometres from Guisborough, although I assume it's difficult for her to go and see plays if she doesn't understand the language.

I was arrested on 9 November in the evening, and after a long and humiliating night during which we had to clean the streets of Berlin with toothbrushes, we were taken to a re-education school just east of Berlin. We were woken up every morning at 5 a.m. and had to go through endless roll-calls until 7 or 8 in the morning. The temperatures were never higher than −3 or −2 degrees. We were only given something to eat at noon, and that wasn't much. This whole thing played havoc with my diabetes; I used to faint three or four times a day. This went on for three weeks. Then one day they called me and some others in. After standing for five hours outside an office, an SS officer came and announced that all we 'dirty Jews' could go home. He made it clear that they would give us six weeks to get out of Germany. If, by then, we hadn't left, we would be rearrested. Next time he said it wouldn't be a holiday camp like it was this time …

Now I'm so sorry that I didn't get out before, when you told me to come with you, but then I thought how stupid you were to do what you were doing – putting your whole family through such a traumatic situation, uprooting them from their home and friends, to bring them to a strange country where they didn't speak the language. If it had been London, maybe one could have compared it to Leipzig. But to bring them to a place that no one had ever heard of that couldn't even be found on the map! At the time I said to Mama that it wasn't only foolish but that it was also cruel. Mama had said in any case that the entire situation would blow over in a short time and we'll only remember it as a bad dream. Now Mama and I must do whatever we can to get out of here, and as soon as we can.

I'm writing this letter to you in despair, asking if you could find any way to get us a permit to enter England. We've tried Switzerland, where as you know, Aunt Sarah, Mama and Uncle David have a cousin. Although she was prepared to give us a guarantee, the Swiss authorities wouldn't let us enter. Now because of a new law that we have to have a 'J' stamped in our passports, it isn't possible to cross the border into Switzerland. We've tried France, Italy, Palestine and Romania, but with no luck. You are our last hope. If you can't do anything for us, we'll be sent to the East, like the Polish Jews in October. With Mama's old age and me with my diabetes, we wouldn't survive.

Mama and I have decided that if I can get the necessary papers to come to England, we'll pack up all our belongings and send them on to Middlesbrough. Then I'll start working and do all I can to send for Mama to follow.

Mama is sending her love, and give my love to all.

Adolf

Zelig Schmulewitsch arranged an entry permit for Adolf and secured a guarantor for him. He was to be brought in as a sewing machine technician, but it proved difficult to obtain a permit for Lina. She was too old and she did not have a profession that was a relevant trade category to get into England (she was a hat-decorator); nor did she have the necessary £500.

The following letter is from Adolf's sister Berta to her mother and brother in Leipzig.

Letters

Cetata Alba
15 February 1939

Dear Mama and Adolf,
Much has changed here, mostly since the November pogrom. Although Siyoma did find a new job as an agricultural adviser in one of Baron Hirsh's training farms, and that has compensated us for the loss of the meat outlet we had, he thinks it's wrong to send Jewish people from Europe to Argentina to exploit the Indian tribes, as much as it's wrong what Baron Rothschild and the Zionists are doing in Palestine to the Arabs. But he likes the work. It always seems to me that he gets on better with animals than with people.

Lately when he comes home he starts these big arguments with me or his brothers about workers' rights. I find it somewhat ironic that a person who comes from such a well-to-do family, with servants and peasants, goes out of his way to protect the workers. But I don't have any more *koyach* [strength] to argue with him; he always resorts to physical violence when he doesn't agree with me. We've lost most of our friends and gained quite a few enemies in the last few years due to his views on Bolshevism. Sometimes I think of how we met through the Leipzig communist cell at the university, and how he had impressed me with his opinions about freedom for the workers, equality to all mankind and a better world for our children. But then I was only 19 years old. Today I can see it was all a load of rubbish. He has endless rows with his brothers about socialism, not so much about the ideology, but they blame him for the shame he brought onto the family because of the way he spread his ideas around the town. Miron, his older brother, the one who is the mayor, says it puts him in an awkward position.

These three German women that I told you about have stopped sending their children to me for German lessons. I heard that they had received threats from local Nazi party activists, just after the November pogrom, warning them not to have any contact with Jews. So, for the only people I have anything in common with, I'm a Jew. For the Romanians, I'm a German. For the Jews, I'm a communist. For Siyoma I'm a capitalist. For the rest of his family I'm a snob and for myself, I don't know who I am.

I'm starting to get the 'pension rooms' ready for the spring guests who'll start coming for the swimming season in April.

11

Adolf, I really hope that this job with 'Bellow Engineering' in England will work out so that Mama will be able to follow you there shortly. I still think that if you and Mama came here it would be better for all of us. However bad the situation is here, we're not under the threat of war like in Czechoslovakia, England and France. But it's your choice, and as I always say, 'you have to make your bed and lie in it', and I hope you'll be happy. I miss you all, and don't forget to give my love to the Witleses before they leave for Palestine, particularly my dear friend Naomi.

Siyoma and Judith send their love. I miss you and Leipzig so much.

20 February 1939

As you can see I haven't sent the letter, as something fairly interesting came up on the day I went to the post. Do you remember in 1927, when Siyoma was at the final stage of his studies and was thinking of accepting a teaching post in the University, when he got a letter from some well-known chemistry scientist from Manchester University by the name of Weizmann? In the letter this Dr Weizmann was pleading with him to come and be part of a team of scientists, agronomists and teachers that would establish a Hebrew university for Jewish students in Palestine. They were then thinking of opening a school for agriculture, and they wanted Siyoma to organize it and be the head of it. Siyoma didn't take it seriously, saying that the idea of a Zionist movement – that all Jews should come and live in Palestine – was preposterous. He had said that it would be much better if all the Jews went and lived in the land of the workers (the Soviet Union), and help build a new world.

Yesterday when he came home from work he told me that a French Jew from the agriculture school in Toulouse, a Dr Wolkovich, had visited them on the farm, and offered him a teaching post in the agriculture department of this university. He told him that although most of the campus is in Jerusalem, the school for farming was outside in a small village by the name of Rehovot. Siyoma rejected this proposal outright, saying that it was beneath him to go and live in a place where there was only wilderness and Arabs; but more to the point, he's an expert in cattle, not camels. But it's interesting to think that ten years ago who would

12

have thought that anything would come out of it, and now there in Jerusalem, a place we only mention round the Passover table and hear about in synagogue, there's a university for Jewish people, teaching in Hebrew – a language only our forefathers used to speak. Maybe this is the sign that the *moshiach* [Messiah] is on his way and we should all pack up and take our belongings and go to Palestine, before it's too late. Don't be concerned! I haven't become religious or a Zionist or any other 'ist', but somewhere in the back of my mind I do think that with all this anti-Semitism in Germany, now flooding the whole of Europe, it could strike at us Jews, at a time and a place and with a force that we've never known before. Wouldn't it be better if we could all live in a country that would only be for Jews?

Love,
Berta

In order for Adolf to travel to England he needed a visa to enable him to travel through Holland so he could then take a ferry from Rotterdam to Newcastle.

He wrote the following letter (in German) to the Dutch embassy in Berlin:

Humboldtstrasse 3
1 March 1939

I am writing to enquire about the procedure and cost of obtaining a visa to pass through Holland. I am emigrating to England and have an English visa that is effective until 1 January 1940. I am considered a stateless person and have permission to leave Germany until 30 June 1939.

From the information that I received here in Leipzig, I understand that I can get a transit visa at the Dutch border and would not have to pay.

As I don't wish to have any difficulties on the journey, and I also don't want to lose either time or money, please inform me how I can get through Holland by the quickest route possible, so that I can get to my work in England.

I am enclosing a return stamp.

Thanking you in advance.

Yours faithfully,
Adolf Rochman

The answer read:

The Dutch Embassy
Berlin

We hereby give you a certificate that allows you to enter Holland within the next three weeks through the Krefeld border crossing and exit from Rotterdam harbour. You are not allowed to remain in Holland over the three-week period.

Adolf arrived in England in March 1939. He wrote the following letter to his mother, who was still in Leipzig.

Middlesbrough
Saturday, 25 March 1939

Dear Mama,

I'm sorry that I haven't had the opportunity to write before. I've been so busy trying to get things sorted out. I had a long talk with Bellow to see what can be done in order to get a visa and permit for you. That in itself wasn't easy as he couldn't speak a word of German. Berta[3] had to come along and translate for me. It is funny how people here can only speak English. At home most people could speak Yiddish, Polish or something else, not *goyim* of course, but he's a Jew. Bellow suggested that the best thing is to put the case into the hands of a lawyer. He doesn't have the time to deal with it. In other words it seems as if he's saying 'I have other responsibilities and I can't be bothered with this.' I guess he's thinking that he's done his duty by getting me the papers and the visa. He also suggested that I should change my name. He's right: to go around this country at a time like this with a name like Adolf isn't a good idea. I decided to adopt the name of Peter – do you remember it was the name we gave the rubber boat that we used when we went to the water polo competitions. It's a funny feeling. At first I didn't respond when people called me Peter, thinking that they were talking to someone else, but I'm slowly getting used to it.

Aunt and Uncle are busy trying to find their way in this new country. They think that they can't do anything that is

---

3. A cousin living in Middlesborough.

unorthodox; anything that would anger their English neighbours. Every morning Uncle and Max go to the factory in the nearby town, Guisborough, 15 kilometres down the road. Herman is in London, working as the firm's representative for the south of England. Berta is the work manager on the factory floor. At the same time she's taking care of her family and doing all she can to get Jack's parents out. What I'm trying to say is that they've left me to deal with the permits and papers we need in order to get the visa for you to come here. The first problem is that I don't know my way around; I don't know to whom and where to go. Worst of all, my English isn't good enough. Secondly, I don't have enough money to pay a lawyer, so I couldn't give him the case to deal with anyway.

I hope that sometime soon I'll go down to London, get the jewellery from Dina[4] and pawn it. With some of the money I'll get myself a place to live, and the rest I'll use to pay for a lawyer.

The news from Czechoslovakia is very worrying. Here people say that they could have told Neville Chamberlain that Hitler wouldn't keep his promise. For anyone that comes from the Old Country it doesn't seem astonishing that the Wehrmacht have occupied Prague. The English can only think of it as 'Hitler didn't play fair.' Somehow they think that this whole thing that's happening in Europe is no more than some sort of big cricket game.

I feel well and it's a wonderful feeling to feel free. It's a feeling that I cannot describe. But I have some health problems. I think that it's from the food, which I'm not used to yet.

I really hope that within two or three weeks we'll be together again. I just know that you'll love England, although you'll think that people are a bit strange. You may have some problems learning English, but if Aunt Sarah learned, you will too.

I'm longing to see you again very soon.

Love, Adolf

---

4. Mrs Dina Thorn was a woman who had smuggled Lina's jewellery out of Germany so that Adolf could sell it when he arrived in England. The intention had been to use the money to try to pay for a lawyer and a visa to get Lina out of Leipzig.

This following letter from Lina was written in Yiddish on Adolf's old headed paper.

Adolf Rochman
Insurance Agent Leipzig C-1
Humboldtstrasse 3
Leipzig
Saturday, 15 April 1939

Dear Adolf,

Why are you complaining about your health? Are you unhealthy because you're not eating enough? Or is it because you're eating things that you shouldn't? Why don't you go to the doctor? Do you take your injections regularly? I know that you're eating things that you shouldn't; you should take more care. You could eat cucumbers with sour cream; you can prepare this yourself without having to cook anything. You could also buy butter as there's no Jewish rationing in England.

I got the rent for the two rooms from Fritz but there's still a hundred marks due. Is that his debt? Ask Aunt Sarah what sort of a common family he comes from, and she'll tell you some stories about him.

When the things arrive you shouldn't give anything away until I get there, so that I can see for myself what we need and what we can sell or give away. Now I'm sorry that we sent all my clothes. It's still quite cold here and I only have the one dress to wear. My shoes are getting worn out. (I try to do as much walking as I can, so that I'll look good when I have to go to the consul to get my visa.) I'm sure that they'll last for a week or two until I get to England though. What you must remember is that when I arrive and you come and meet me at the boat, you must bring my red dress and the black shoes with you. I'll have to change before getting off the boat. I don't want anyone to see me in this old rag that I'm wearing now.

On Thursday 13 [April], Herman Uko and his young wife Ayala left for Palestine. Somehow they got a certificate. You know that Herman's father was well off before the bad times, and I think he bought land in Palestine about ten years ago. Herman told me it's in some place in the north, not far from a big city in Lebanon, I think he said somewhere with a 'B' – Babelon, Beirut, or something like that. I never know with these biblical Arab names: what they mean and how you should pronounce them, let alone remember their names. To me they all sound the same. He did say that it wasn't far from another port city which is on a big mountain. The only thing I can remember about it is that it has something to do with the prophet Elijah – the one we open the door for and give a cup of wine to on Pesach. Ayala said that in this city 'Hif' or 'Hifel', or something like that, there are a lot of former Leipzigers who have come to live there in the last five years. I met him in the community centre when I came to collect your letter. (By the way you should know that all the letters that are sent to Jews come to the community headquarters where they are looked over by the Gestapo before we get them. You must be more careful with what you write, or write in Yiddish.) In Palestine, they're going to drain the swamps. As he told me that, his eyes shone, as if they were going to America to find gold. I'm glad that I don't have to go with them. It seems to me that, bad as it is here, it's evidently worse there, with all the Arabs, deserts, swamps, malaria, camels and God knows what other calamities. They're due to arrive in about three months. He gave you his regards and he also said to tell you that he's very upset that you didn't answer his letter.

Dear Adolf, could Aunt Sarah get me out of here as a housemaid? She needs no money for that. Do you think I've nothing to do all day? Everyday, from morning to night, we have to go and work in some sort of a munitions factory. We don't get paid, and we have to walk to the factory. Sometimes they give us some food, but usually the strong and young get to it first, so I stay hungry. I have so many troubles – I don't know where to start.

'The stateless' have to move out of their homes that are in Aryan areas by the first of May, to move to 'Jewish homes'. I don't know what to do with the rest of the furniture. No one will buy it, and I can't lift it all or take it with me. Most of the people who rent rooms in the 'Jewish homes' zone are very primitive; they don't let us into the kitchen, even if it's only to prepare something to eat. I just don't know where to get money to pay the rent for this move. I've no money for food, let alone for heat, rent and stamps. I just feel totally lost. Luckily I met Paul Niederland, a teacher in the Jewish school. He and his family will be leaving for France next week and he'll take my letter and post it from there. I do get six marks a week from the community and one ration of oil which I usually can't cook with, so I put it on the bread. The only bread we get is five or six days old. You must ask Aunt

Sarah if she could send me some butter.

Dear Adolf, I think the best thing to do at this point is to put an announcement in the Middlesbrough local newspaper to get work for me. Maybe you can ask people on the Jewish Committee if they need someone to work for them. I don't want to come and live under Uncle Zelig's wing. We did this once, do you remember just after father died in Humboldtstrasse 23? I would like to get off the boat in Newcastle and start working the next day.

Dear Adolf, I don't understand, are you so busy that you can't find any time to do these things for me? You haven't told me anything about the furniture. Did it arrive safely? What have you done with it? You must do something so that the moths don't eat everything up. Go and buy some mothballs, give them to the movers and tell them to roll the carpet open, put them in and then roll the whole thing back again. Don't open the boxes before I come. Did you get the money and jewellery from this *zezkey* [tart] of yours – Mrs Dina Thorn? Did she run away with our property? Why don't you write about this? You must give me an answer when I ask you something. All these things such as you changing your name is of no interest to me. I don't care that you changed it – that's up to you. For me you'll always be Adolf. You'd better spend more of your time and effort on writing and telling me things that are important.

Adolf, don't forget me here; don't leave me in Leipzig. You must get me out; anyway that you can. Don't let them send me to the East.

I've no more room to write so I'll stop here.

Love from your sad Mama

The following letter was written in Yiddish by Lina to her brother, David Oberman. He had arrived in England from Leipzig in 1938 and was working as an accountant in London. The letter was sent to Adolf, who forwarded it to David Oberman.

Leipzig
Thursday, 13 April 1939

This is the third letter that I've written to you. And you still haven't bothered to answer me. I also gave Adolf a letter to give to you, which I think that you must have got by now. But I've still heard nothing. Aren't I your sister? The closest relative that you have? David, we are all Obermans, and we have to help each other. Don't you know that I must get out of Leipzig? I have a permit to stay here for only another month. If I don't get out by then they'll send me to the East, as they did the Polish Jews.

I know that Adolf is trying his best to get a visa for me, and that Sarah and Zelig are helping too, but as yet nothing has come out of all their efforts. Time is running out. Since Heydrich took over the Bureau of Jewish Affairs at the end of last month, things are getting worse. Every day, sometimes every hour, there are new decrees, injunctions and regulations about what Jews are or are not allowed to do, eat, talk, read, buy, sell, listen to, travel in, or visit. There are so many and they come so often that most of my time is spent going around trying to find out what the new restrictions are that have been published during the day. Of course they don't tell you these on the radio, as Jews aren't allowed to listen to or for that matter own a wireless, but they paste them on the walls of Jewish homes. If you happen to be passing then you'll see – otherwise they punish you, mostly by beating, for violation of the laws of the Fatherland. The other day I found out that, starting from the 15 April, a Jew won't be allowed to buy chocolate. Not that I was thinking of buying any, it's too expensive for me, but I ask why? And why starting from the 15th? The result will be that on the 16th or 17th, Jewish homes will be raided by the Brown or the Black – or some other colour – Shirts, looking for chocolate that the Jews will supposedly be hiding in their kitchens. At the same time, they will confiscate, thieve, rob and pilfer other things that they fancy in the house, or what's left from the last time they came. I've not even mentioned the beatings, slappings and rape that they perform, if they find a woman who is to their liking. If you dare complain to the police, or the Gestapo, the first thing they do is arrest you for defying the honour of an Aryan, because you've said that he slept with a Jewish woman, or what they call an *Untermensch* [subhuman], and then they may send you to the East. What's worse is that from the little money I have, or what is sent to me by Zelig or Berta, they take 20 per cent before they give it to me; that's in order to repay them for the damage that the Jews caused on the night of the big pogrom in November.

David, I'm an old woman, and I don't have many years to live; you must do something to get me out of this hell. If I'm sent to the East – and remember they can do this as a punishment for the smallest offence, like not moving off the pavement when an Aryan comes along – that will be the end of me. I will never see Adolf again, and I'll perish there, in one of those small villages beyond the dark mountains.

David, save me. I'm sure that you're able to do so.

Your loving sister,
Lina

Adolf received the following letter from his mother.

Dear Adolf,
I did tell you didn't I that you should ask David about what I asked you? If you won't ask him, I just don't know what I'll do.

How are things with you and your health? Do you belong to a health insurance group? You must see to it that you don't eat things that you shouldn't. You shouldn't drink too much; you could buy yourself some Cognac and drink that if you feel thirsty. I don't see any problem in you eating cucumber with cream; this is, after all something which you can prepare yourself. You shouldn't go swimming. I don't sleep at night – I'm completely distraught about all these things. How do you eat? Do you have all your things with you? Do you think you need an overall? I can send one from here if you want.

I'll need a suitcase in order to pack all the things I would like to bring to England. I only have a basket and that won't become me if I arrive with it – I don't want Aunt Sarah and Uncle Zelig to see me in my poverty. But I don't have any money for this. What do you think I should do? What's happened with the mover? He said that he hasn't received any money and also that he didn't get the money from the insurance, which he said he had to pay from his own pocket, and so now I'll have to pay him with something from our possessions. If not I'll have to get new documents. My permit to stay in Leipzig is expiring, and I must get a new one that costs some ten marks. I don't know where I'll get the money for this.

Dear Adolf, do you think I should bring a paraffin cooker with me as I don't know how to cook on a gas cooker?

I'm sending you all the documents from the passport bureau, so you'll have all the papers in hand when you go to collect the visa for me. I must have them back soon.

Dear Adolf, you must send me an answer to all my questions. Again, I beg you to go to Uncle David, because if you don't, I don't see how I'll be able to get out of this furnace.

I love you as always. Don't forget me.

Mama

Having received his sister Lina's desperate letter, David Oberman sent this reply to Adolf:

London
Monday, 24 April

Dear Adolf,
Thank you for your letter which I received this morning. I'm glad to hear that things are going well for you and I think that you'll learn the language in a short time. I also stayed at the 'Grey House' for a short time after I arrived; it seems as if it's a station for all Leipzigers that come over.

As for your mother, I've spoken to a lawyer here in London and he said that he'll try to do his best, but of course he won't do it for free. In addition he said that your mother's case isn't easy. She's not in any of the categories that are required by the Home Office to grant her an entry visa. She's over the proper age, has no profession (a hat-decorator isn't a required trade), she's a sick person, comes from an enemy country, has no money to cover her expenses and I can't find an English person who will vouch for her. When you try to talk to people about this, they say that 'the Germans that have come over here have caused us enough anti-Semitism as it is'. What's more is that they can't see what is so desperate about the situation.

What I think we should do is somehow gather all the money resources that we have (and maybe Max or Herman will chip in as well), get a good lawyer with good contacts in the Home Office, and see what he can do. By the way, the woman that I'm seeing now works for the lawyer that I told you about. So you must send me the papers that Lina sent to you.

I'll wait for a letter from you and then we can get on and deal with this matter.

Love,
Uncle David

Lotti Katz arrived in England with her family in May 1939. Her brother, Carol, later married Shnoki (Yette) Schmulewitsch, who was Adolf's cousin. Lotti's father had not wanted his son to marry the daughter of a stateless Eastern European Jew and thought that his son had lost his legal career because of this. Carol and Lotti Katz owned a toyshop.

W. Hartlepool
Sunday, 9 May 1939

Dear Adolf ,
Yette came to see my brother on Shabbes, and I was thrilled to hear that you had arrived and were staying with them in Middlesbrough. Why didn't you tell me that you'd arrived? The last time I heard from you, you mentioned your plans to leave Leipzig sometime in March, and that on your way to Holland you would stop in Kassel whilst waiting for the train. But I presumed something had happened with the Gestapo or God knows what, and you couldn't make it. Anyway I was so relieved to hear that you had got out.

I've been through such a lot since the last time we met in Leipzig.

You remember that my father was honoured with an Iron Cross from the war? So we all hoped, or should I say wanted to believe, that we were safe. Even when they threw out the Polish Jews, we didn't feel any threat. Father would say, 'We don't have to worry, we're German and they won't touch us.' Also, if you remember, he was furious with Carol, who had left two years ago. Of course he liked to ignore the fact that Jewish lawyers weren't allowed to practise law any longer. For him nothing had changed, and no matter what Kate[5] and I tried to point out to him, he was of the opinion that it was only a passing phenomenon. Things changed very radically after the pogrom. Then not only did he lose his position in the town council but he was also arrested. When he came home from prison, which was more or less

---

5. Kate was Lotti and Carol's sister.

the same time that you came home, he decided that we had to leave.

Luckily for us he had some contacts, so he could get visas for all of us to leave, and even luckier was that Carol was in England and could arrange work permits for us here. My father arranged for all three of us to go on the Portuguese train. We stayed in Lisbon for some time, until Carol finalized our papers, and two weeks ago we landed in W. Hartlepool. In the meantime things aren't easy: Father has no work and is feeling very humiliated because of what happened, and not knowing or understanding one word of English doesn't help things. You can imagine how he feels after having had his own law firm, where language is the most important tool that you work with.

I presume you know how they squeezed every pfennig out of us. So at the moment we're living with Carol in one room at the back of the store. After living in a big house it brings a lot of tension, particularly between Carol and Father, who still treats him as if he was the youngest child. Last week Mama and I started working for some English people, cleaning houses. Father finds this difficult to cope with.

My sister, by the way, who planned to leave a day before us, somehow got on the wrong boat, and landed in Brazil. We were astonished that she wasn't in Hartlepool when we arrived and Carol hadn't heard from her either. But just yesterday we received a letter telling us about her whole ordeal.

It's just terrible what Hitler and his mob has done to us.

But in any case I must stop complaining. After all we are safe and sound now, and there are people who are in a worse situation than we are. By the way, what's happening with your mother? Is she already here? Or is she still on the way?

Adolf, what can I tell you? It was just wonderful to hear that you aren't far away and I do hope we can meet as soon as possible.

Loving you as always,
Lotti

By the first week of May, Adolf had received most of his papers so that he could begin work. He moved into a bedsit in Leeds where other German refugees lived. Later in May, he received this letter from his mother.

Leipzig
Saturday, 13 May

Dear Adolf,

On Thursday, thank goodness, I got a message that they came to pick up the furniture with a lorry that has now come and gone and is now on its way to Chemnitz. When it arrives, with God's help, you must immediately find a room and store all the things in it. Remember to put mattresses on the floor and the furniture above. You must check that everything is there. Take someone to check it with you and then close it immediately. Don't unpack the wash-kit in the big suitcase; wait until I arrive.

I can't cook in the room. They don't let me. When I need water I have to take it from the toilet bowl. Adolf, I'll never live through this. I can't go to the Witlese's every time I need some hot water. They're not the best of people. I'm withering away from *tsores* [troubles].

Now we, I mean those over 50, have to go and work in the garbage site every day for hours on end. We earn six marks from the [Jewish] Committee so that we then have something to live off. We work there from morning till night, sorting out the rubbish. The only thing that's good about it is that sometimes I can find food. That's the only thing that's keeping me alive. But the work is very hard; I get cold and it has ruined my shoes. Maybe I'll find something to put on my feet. It's forbidden to take, but the German in charge is kind and sometimes allows us to take things and even to work sitting down, as long as there are no Gestapo inspectors around.

You mustn't tell Uncle and Aunt what I've told you; no one must ever know that I work in a garbage dump. I don't want to imagine what they'll think when I come over.

Please write to Uncle David and tell him that I'm starving, if it's not already clear. If I don't get money for the rent for the room, you'll soon not have to trouble yourself about me anymore.

Your loving Mama

Adolf's sister Berta sent him the following highly reproachful letter:

Hadrian St 50
Cetata Alba
Monday, 15 May 1939

Dear Adolf,
Today I received a letter from Mama, claiming that I'd
spoken about you in a very bad way. In spite of the fact that
you haven't seen any reason to write, even a postcard, and
in spite of the fact that I'm older than you, I'll make the first
move and write to you. I had written that letter when I was
in a bad mood after I'd received a letter from Mama telling
me that she didn't know where to find you. Adolf, didn't
you see the need to write to us, or to Mama for that matter?
Mama has lost her house because of you and now she has to
go from one family to the next, living in servant's quarters
with five or six men and women in the same room, and no
money to live off. If Mama had stayed in the Humboldtstrasse 3 house, she wouldn't have needed help. It's awful
that she has to live with the Witleses in a horrible room, in
what was once servants' quarters. The thought of Mama
living in it breaks my heart. Often I think about what's
happened to all of us and it makes me cry. Mostly I think of
Mama. You must understand that I didn't write what I wrote
in order to hurt you.
    I do understand that to live and care for an old mother
isn't easy. I know that I've written about this before, but I
can only ask you again: do something to get Mama out.
From here in Romania, I can't do a thing. But if Mama stays
much longer in Leipzig, she won't survive. I can't go there
because I don't have the money and in any case I can't get
the travel papers to enter Germany as a Jew.
    Where's all the furniture? Where's the silver? Where's
the piano?
    How's your health? What are you studying? What are
your plans? Wouldn't it be better to marry into a respectable
family? By doing so you'll be able to get on in life. That's
what many young people seem to be doing today.
    How's Dora? How's Herman? I don't hear from them
any more. Has everyone forgotten me?
    I don't feel well; my heart is bad and my nerves are gone.
I've also got bad rheumatism.
    Judith's a big girl now, she'll soon be twelve. She'll be
going to high school. She's a good student and is very slim
and beautiful.

That's all I can say from our side. Please don't let things go on as they are. Do something so that Mama can get a visa before it's too late.

I hope all will go well for you and I hope that God grants you health and prosperity.

From your loving sister,
Berta

Later on that summer, Adolf received two more desperate letters from his mother:

Leipzig
Saturday, 15 July 1939

Dear Adolf,
It's a long time since you've written to me. Have you forgotten that you have a mother who is completely trapped here; who can't get out; who has nothing to eat and nowhere to live? Write to me immediately and tell me if Mr Bellow can help me get out of this hell. He could claim that he needs me as a housemaid and so I would need to come quickly.

If I don't get out by the end of the month they'll throw me out of here. They're preparing for war. All over town there are soldiers; more and more of the Jewish homes round by the railway station are being taken over so that they'll have rooms for their officers. If a *milchoma* [war] happens, I'll never get out of here.

Dear Adolf, help me, write to me and tell me what I should do? Tell me that everything will be OK.

17 July

I've just come back from the Gestapo headquarters. After a long humiliating wait, during which I had to stand on my feet for over four hours, the man gave me a permit to stay here until 1 August. He said, or I should say he barked at me, that if I and the 'other dirty Jews' haven't left by then that no extension on our visas will be granted. If I'm not out by then they'll send me to Poland, like all the others. The extension cost 15 marks. I had to borrow it from the Witleses. Now I don't have any more money to buy food for this week. The work at the garbage site is killing me. It hurts my hands and has ruined my shoes. Last week I found a sock and I put it on straight away so at least I could have one warm foot.

Dear Adolf, I'm so miserable and tired. I won't last here much longer. Maybe you could send me some sort of certificate that I could show to the Gestapo. I could prove that I have a permit to come to England and that it's only a matter of time until I get a visa.

I heard the *goyim* say that when Goebbels was in Leipzig two weeks ago, he'd said that if Poland doesn't allow the unification of Danzig and continues to be aggressive, there'll only be cemeteries left in Poland. He also said that the Jews, with their worldwide 'network of subversion and conspiracy' are pushing the two peace-loving countries to war.

Dear Adolf, if the Jews are so powerful and influential as he said, why can't they get me out of here?

Take care of yourself – don't eat what you shouldn't. Remember you're completely on your own now; I'm not with you to look after you. Drink Cognac. Stay healthy. I will see you soon.

Your loving Mama

Leipzig
Saturday, 2 September 1939

Dear Adolf,
I've run out of your letterheaded paper from the insurance firm; this is the only paper I could find, so forgive me for writing in this way. The pencil you left me is now so blunt that I can hardly write with it anymore.

Did you get a letter from Berta? Did she tell you that I don't have one pfennig? Did she send you a package of food. Don't give anyone anything out of it.

Adolf, I'm completely in despair. I've asked for money from anywhere and anyone I can think of. I've been given six marks from the Committee. What shall I do with it? Every time I go there I have to fill in these forms. It's so humiliating to have to stand at the door with all the beggars; to go from one clerk to another, just to receive my money for working at the garbage site. Can you send me some money or some food, even just ten shillings, so that I can buy a new pencil and a postage stamp? Write to Uncle David and tell him to send me some butter, so I'll have some fat on my bones. I'm enclosing an envelope so that you can write your new address on it.

Dear Adolf, when do you think that I'll get the visa? I must get out of this room, and I don't want to get another if the permit is coming in a day or two. This room is the most terrible place to live in. I could only wish it on my worst enemy.

Dear Adolf, I was so excited to hold your letter; it was waiting for me when I came back from work today and I couldn't stop crying. Don't leave my case in someone else's hands. Do it yourself and do all you can or I'll never get out of here. My dear Adolf, I'm a healthy woman and not as old as people think. I can work and I'd like to earn money. You could put an advertisement in the paper for a service girl, a cook, or even a housemaid. Say I'm a woman of fifty – you don't have to say that I'm older. Call the Committee and tell them I can work with old people or with children. I can even look after sick people in hospital – I did it during the Great War. I'm sure that you'll have so many offers you won't know what to do with them. Go there today and tell them. Adolf, don't be ashamed; tell them I'm your mother. I'm sure that they'd love to have me as a worker.

I got a letter from Berta. She told me that there's no chance of getting into Romania. She said that they're throwing out all the *staatenlos* [stateless]. It's a good thing that she and Judith have got their Romanian passports. At least they're safe.

I was thinking that I could walk to the Swiss border at Bregenz. Do you think it would take me more than five days? They say that if you have an entry visa there's no difficulty in getting in. What do you think of that plan? Adolf, you must go straight away to the Swiss consul in London and see if you can get this visa for me. I don't think that you'll have any problem in getting it; you only have to make sure that there'll be someone in England that can give a guarantee. Once I have this, the Swiss police won't worry that I'll be staying there too long. Dear Adolf, you must write to Aunt Sarah today. Tell her that I can't live like this; she must send me a guarantee via the Swiss consul.

Dear Adolf, I hope that you're looking after yourself. Who prepares your food for you? Don't eat fatty things. Tell Aunt that I said that she should cook for you and send it over. How's the work? Don't work too hard. Do you understand?

Dear Adolf, don't forget me here. I'll perish if I don't get out soon. Dear Adolf, if you have an ounce of mother love in you, you'll see to it that I get out of here before it's too late.

You must be my protector.

Dear Adolf, with all my tensions and *tsores*, I've forgotten your birthday. So, I bless you for good health, luck and long life.

Love,
your Mama

In September Adolf received a letter from his cousin Dora (daughter of the Schmulewitsches) in Guisborough.

Guisborough
14 September 1939

Dear Adolf,

It's Rosh Hashanah today, and as Yom Kippur is on its way Mama and I decided to take some time off to try and answer all the people we owe letters to. After all, we'd like to find favour in HIS eyes.

There's no need to be so angry about Aunt Lina. We didn't answer her as we lost her address; she's moved so often that it is impossible to keep track of where she is. Why didn't she stay in Humboldtstrasse 3 until she got her papers to leave? You should know that we, and particularly Mama, are doing all we can to see that her sister can get a visa to come over.

We're very happy that you like your new job with Bellow's. It does give you the option of making more money than working for us. I always say that it's better not to work for your family – there are too many conflicting interests – and Max says that working for us is no career for you.

Father and Max don't have anything against Bellow. For that matter they do very much appreciate the fact that he did so much to get you out. I don't see why he doesn't show any interest in trying to get this visa for Aunt Lina though? After all it's only one or two letters to people he knows and the thing can be arranged. Max and Herman both think that he could have given us a better price on the sewing machines; after all we are *mishpocha* [family].

I'm glad you've dealt with the business with that terrible woman without going to court. I hope that you'll have *mazel* [luck] and that you'll get the things soon.

From here there's not much news.

Last night I went to a dance that was organized by the

synagogues in Middlesbrough. It was quite nice but most of the men were from the *Kinder* and they're much too young for me. It seems to me that Shnoki will marry; after all she's always with this Katz man. That is in spite of Father's objection. Father doesn't like Carol because he always looks down on us *Ostjuden*. His family are from the Alreich, therefore he thinks that he's better than us. In any case Max says that she's only nineteen and too young to get married. I say that if she wants to get married so much, she should find someone of her own kind.

Business could be somewhat better, especially as the winter season is coming up. Father had hoped that with the war going on now that there would be more need for uniforms and army clothing. But one mustn't complain, things could be worse.

What do you say about the little bastard attacking Poland? Do you think that'll last? I think Britain should put an end to it as soon a possible.

Herman is still in London and he's been ill for sometime now.

Mama received a letter from this lawyer, Kohn. In it he suggested a way to get Aunt Lina's visa, but he wants over £100 for his services. Mama thinks that it's too much. In any case, she says the whole thing will soon be over, but she was thinking of going to see if she can get him to lower his price. If not, tell him we don't need his favours, and we can manage the whole thing by ourselves. It's amazing how many sly people come out of the woodwork when they think that there's money to be made from other people's misery.

If the war doesn't disrupt things too much, we're planning to come to Leeds on 15 November. If we do, we'll bring the shirt you forgot in Middlesbrough.

So I hope to see you soon.

Lots of love,
Dora

The following letter is from Adolf's sister Berta in Romania to her cousin Berta (daughter of the Schmulewitsches) living in Middlesbrough.

Cetata Alba
Sunday, 15 October [1939]

Dear Berta,

I'm writing to you as you're our last chance. All the letters that I've sent to Aunt Sarah and Uncle Zelig have been useless. As I'm sure you've guessed, I'm writing about my mother. I received a letter from her the other day which I'm sending on to you, and then you can judge for yourself the poor and miserable situation that she's in. We've done all we can from our side to try and get her out. It's just impossible – they're not letting anyone in. Everyday there are thousands of Jews trying to come in – from Poland, Czechoslovakia, Galicia and God only knows from where else. The only ones that they let in are people who have a visa to go on to Palestine. They're putting them in a concentration camp in Constastza [Constanta] until a ship comes to pick them up. We had some of them come through here. They were telling hair-raising stories about what the Gestapo are doing. It's difficult to believe everything that they said – maybe they're only saying these things to get our sympathy – but if only a quarter of what they said is true, I can only thank God that we're safe here. Now that Judith and I have got our Romanian papers, there's no way that they can deport us, as they are doing to people who came here in the last five or six years. But we still feel the war. It's said that Bolshevik troops are amassing on the other side of the border, along the Dniester. The Soviets are threatening that they'll take over the whole of Romania if the king doesn't give up Moldavia.

In any case that's not why I'm writing. It's about Mama. I don't understand. Don't you have a heart? Isn't she your aunt? Don't you know how serious the situation is? Do you and your parents know what's happening over there? I would have done more for your mother if the situation had been in reverse. You and I know very well that if you or Uncle Zelig had done half of what's been done in order to get your parents-in-law out, Mama would have been safe long ago. Is it because I married a communist and so you can't forgive me? I'll tell you this: I personally need nothing from you or your family. As far as I'm concerned, you can carry on living your smug life, but if you don't see to it that my mother gets out – and now – I'll never forgive you.

Berta

The next letter is from Lotti Katz, in Hartlepool, to Adolf, now in Leeds.

Hartlepool
Tuesday, 31 October 1939

Dear Adolf,

I never know whether to call you Adolf, or Peter. After all that's the name which is still in my mind – a name that brings back such wonderful memories from back home – but I think you prefer Peter, which seems so strange and removed to me.

Is there any news concerning the whole business with your mother; is the poor woman still stuck there in Leipzig? At least we succeeded in getting out. Both my older sister and her husband escaped to Brazil. Why don't the Schmulewitsches help you? They could at least pay the £100 bond.

Did I tell you that Yette [Shnoki Schmulewitsch] wants to come and live with us in Hartlepool? Max and her father won't hear of it. They said that if she wants to leave home she must get married. You know as well as I do that they oppose it, and that they don't want to have anything to do with us. I wonder how all this will end.

I told my brother and Papa that I needed to go and see the doctor next Saturday; I didn't want them to know that I'm coming to see you. Then I would have to go into a long explanation of why I had to go and see the doctor in Harrogate and why couldn't I go to a doctor in Middlesbrough? Anyway I'll be coming on the 4th, on the 5 p.m. train. I won't be going back until Monday, because of the black-out (trains don't run at night any more). I can't wait to see you on the platform.

You must let me know as soon as possible if this arrangement isn't any good for you. If it isn't, I can make other plans for the Sunday. If we miss one another, I'll wait for you by the gate. If you're going to be busy, I suggest we meet in the same hotel as last time.

Please give me an answer as soon as you can.

The toy business is very slow. We had a short spell of good sales in September, when families were sending their children to the countryside, but since then it has been dead. I think that by Christmas it should pick up again – there's talk that the whole thing will be over by then.

I'm looking forward to seeing you. I just can't wait.

Love,
Lotti

Adolf's reply shows his lack of patience with his family's response to his mother's plight.

Leeds
2 November 1939

Dear Lotti,
I'll wait for you in the station. I only hope that I get there on time. You know what it's like with the fuel restriction. As the buses hardly run it may take me over two hours to walk.

The family are just not interested in my mother's case. In the few letters I get from them, they apologize for not doing anything. I'd prefer that they moved their arses and did something, instead of apologizing all the time. I think that they just don't understand how serious the situation is. They think it's a wave of anti-semitism that will blow over, once this whole thing in Poland is finished and Hitler gets what he wants.

On a more positive note I've got the Committee to register my mother and send an application to Woburn House, so maybe things are moving.

People you talk to over here say that they don't see why 'we should send our boys to fight to a place full of Catholics and Jews'. Most of them don't even know where it is. One of the workers who is a veteran of the Great War told me that 'they should solve their own problems. We have our hands full with the Catholics in Ireland.'

It's funny what you said about my name. My feeling is that there's more than just an official procedure in changing a name. I feel that Adolf associates me with everything that has to do with 'home' and Peter with all that has to do with my new life. Much as I would like to dissociate myself from my former life, it's part of me and always will be. Aren't you the best proof of that? I also find it bewildering that at home we always wanted to integrate and be seen as Germans; but for the Germans we were just Jews. Here, where we're finally identified as Germans, we want to dissociate ourselves from it.

33

It seems that there are many lay-offs in the firm and I could be made redundant. If that happens, I'll go and live in Manchester. They say that there's more work there for Germans.

I look forward to seeing you.

All my love,
Peter

Adolf received another letter from his cousin Dora Schmulewitsch.

Guisborough
Thursday, 30 November

Dear Adolf,
We'd all like to know what's happening with you. We sent a parcel with the shirts. Did you get it? You didn't even send a postcard to say 'thank you'. Mama and Papa would like to know what's happening. Berta got a very nasty letter from your sister in Romania, telling her that neither she or Mama have done anything to help Aunt Lina. As you have all the papers, we don't know what's happening.

Berta said that she thinks that the aunt from Switzerland can get her out, but as far as I know they've not been on speaking terms for years.

We would all really appreciate it if you could stop being so lazy and write us a letter so we know what's happening. Papa said that he's no magician or millionaire who can wave his magic wand and bring Aunt Lina here. You should tell your sister that even here the streets aren't paved with gold. Now with the war going on, we can't do everything we'd like to either. By the way, why doesn't Uncle David [Oberman] do something? After all, he lives in London. Nothing will happen if you don't move your backside. Stop going to the dancing halls every night and spend your time and money on your mother's case. I know that it's easier to give it to someone else to deal with.

How's life in Manchester? Have you made any new friends? Be careful with the women there. They say that northern women are much tougher than us!

I was so upset about Berta's letter that I forgot to tell you the big news; Yette and Carol have announced their marriage. This will be the second marriage in the family since we left home. I don't have to tell you Papa's reaction when he heard it. You know how he hates Germans who always think that they're better than the whole world. The fact that Carol's father has a medal from the Great War doesn't impress him in the least. For him, anyone who doesn't speak Yiddish is at the very least, not a very good person or a *ganif* [thief]. I myself don't see what she sees in this Carol. What is he after all? Not a doctor or a lawyer? Only some third-class *shocher* [merchant] in the *shmata* [cloth] trade. Big deal! I'll send you an invitation once they're printed, but because of the war and rationing it's nearly impossible to get paper. You can talk to those people in the rationing office until you're blue in the face – they just don't care. As if allocating some paper for wedding invitations will change the war!

You must tell us how to reply to Berta.

Love,
Dora

In December Adolf had a letter from an English girlfriend, Anna.

To: Peter Rochman
c/o 3 Hardmas St
Disbury
Manchester 20

3 December 1939

Dear Peter,
Thanks for your letter that arrived this morning. I suppose I should forgive you for not having replied earlier.

Mother wants me to tell you that she received your letter and that she'd be more than pleased to see you on Saturday 9 for the lighting of the third Hanukkah candle. I'm looking forward to your coming. It would be nice if we could go out to the Alderly Edge dance hall. Rolf and Elaine will probably come too, once they know that you'll be there.

If you don't want to come, please tell me as soon as you can by return post – even a postcard will do. Don't forget to tell me what time the bus arrives, so I can wait for you at the bus stop. You say you never see anyone so I thought you might like to have some fun for a change.

I'm disappointed that you're planning to be in

Middlesbrough at Christmas time for the wedding but I do understand that *mishpocha* [family] comes first. I was hoping that you'd be around for the holidays as then we could have had a good time together.

I can't advise you about getting tails or a dinner jacket; I don't even know if you'll be able to afford them. It's not only eight pounds for the shirt but there are extras such as additional white waistcoats, ties, shirts, shoes and silk socks. Tails or dinner jackets are only necessary if the wedding celebration is in the evening. A midday wedding can be with or without a dance reception and then you only need a dark lounge suit.

I honestly can't understand your family in Guisborough. To have such a big wedding party disregarding all the restrictions, at a time like this! A party in a private house is OK, but a big ostentatious wedding doesn't look right nowadays because of the war going on and rationing. I just don't think that they can be too bothered about what the *goyim* could be saying behind their backs. I see no reason to create more anti-Semitism when it's not necessary. I have a lot of friends who got married recently, before their fiancés went over to join the Territorial in France. All these weddings were small quiet celebrations at home.

We're all sorry that you were classified as an enemy alien.

By the way, my brother was recruited the day I came back from Leeds. He's attached to General Gort's 50th Armoured Division. They were all sent over to France. A letter arrived the other day from him. He said that as yet they've not seen any action, but western France, where they are stationed, is beautiful and they're having a good time with the French girls. Rumour is that by Christmas it'll all be over and they'll be sent home. I really do envy those French girls – taking all the Jewish boys. It's just not fair leaving us high and dry here.

I told my father about the problem with your mother. He said that you should bring all the papers you have when you come and he'll see what he can do. There are one or two Czechoslovakian people that he helped get out, so maybe he'll be able to give you some advice on the matter.

Write by return mail.

Can't wait to see you getting off the bus on Saturday night. Nothing more for now.

Love,
Anna

Letters

Later on in December, Adolf wrote to his sister Berta in Romania.

Berta Grusman
55 Trayan St
Cetata Alba
Romania

Thursday, 28 December 1939

Dear Berta,
As you can see I've moved to Manchester. I lost my job in
Leeds and I was offered a better position here, so I think I'll
stay for a while.

Although the war is going on we hardly feel it, except for
the black-outs. But the restrictions on Germans and
Austrians travelling from one city to the next can sometimes
be a nuisance. We need a permit each time we go, but
anyway I don't have the money for travelling, so it doesn't
bother me too much. I would like to go to London though,
just the once, to settle the matter with Mrs Thorn.

From time to time the newspapers are full of reports
about what's happening in Poland, and of course there's
rationing here so you can't get this or that, but it's nowhere
near as bad as it was for us at home before I left. The stories
that are coming out of Poland – what they are doing to the
population, is just hair-raising. I think that if France and
England won't come to Poland's aid as they promised
they'd do, there'll be nothing to stop this madman from
going on and on.

The other day I received a letter from a friend in Palestine;
he'd managed to get there in a sort of roundabout way. He
said that before he left Leipzig the only thing the English
aeroplanes were doing was throwing leaflets down onto the
big cities. In the leaflets there was a warning to Hitler and the
German people that 'it's not a good idea to go to war, and if
they don't pull out of Poland right now they will have to
suffer the consequences'. Apparently the people who do
bother to pick them up just laugh and go on their way.

I'm doing my best for Mama; all I can do is to see to it that
she'll get the visa. I must tell you that I'm standing against a
brick wall. No one is interested, even in Middlesbrough, and
they get irritated every time I bring it up. I tried to talk about
it at the wedding, and Uncle David took me aside and said,
'It's not the right time to bring up such things now.'

I'm learning English quite quickly. I hope that when I've mastered the language a bit better I'll go myself to all these government offices.

How are things between you and Siyoma? Is he still such an austere communist as he was in Leipzig? Or is he prepared to admit that Stalin is not the greatest leader in the world?

Mrs Thorn has still kept the jewellery. She won't let go of it until I promise that I'll marry her and go with her to Australia. I don't know what's worse – to have stayed in Leipzig or to marry that dreadful woman!

I hope that your place, being so close to the Ukraine, won't be run over by the Bolsheviks like in Poland.

I hope that it'll all be over by the spring.

Love,
Adolf/Peter

Adolf received an angry and exasperated reply from Berta:

Sunday, 7 January

Dear Adolf,
After such a long time of not hearing from you I was so glad to get your letter dated 28 December. I don't know what to think about your long silence. I think that it's your complete lack of interest in our family. You're probably feeling irritated that I started this letter with so much criticism against you, but anyway I'm now going to tell you about Mama's situation. She gets six marks a week for working in the garbage site. From that six three goes on rent for the room and one is for heat and so she's left with two marks for food. The room is a hole with no kitchen or place to wash. Mama is begging me in her letter to send her some butter and some money, knowing that there's no place here where I can get foreign money. Besides that, Jews aren't allowed to buy butter or meat. Thank goodness we have some from the farm, but we have to hide it. If they find out that we have any of the restricted foods they'll nationalize the rest of the farm, as they did Siyoma's sister's farm. In her letter Mama told me that the Leipzig Jews are sent to Lublin, some town in former Galicia. Now for some reason they call it Generalgouvernement. They're changing the names every day – I don't know where these places are. We heard, from

38

the Polish refugees coming through here, that they're putting them in open-air camps and letting them freeze to death. Of course one doesn't have to believe every story that comes out of there. I know the Germans better than anyone else and I can tell you that they'd never do a thing like that, in particular not to old people like Mama. But you know Mama's health is very bad; her heart is weak. How would she last the journey from Leipzig to this town, in a third-class compartment?

I'm begging you to do something to get her out, before it's too late. I think if she could get a visa to go to Switzerland maybe she could stay there until the papers came from England. Mama came up with this preposterous idea based on some rumour that she'd heard that it's possible to walk to Dresden, from there to take a train to Prague and walk the rest of the way, through Vienna and Budapest, to Timisoara on the Austrian–Romanian border. She thinks that once she gets there, I can wait for her; she only needs 300 marks to pay for a guide and a border smuggler. She was told that it wouldn't take more than a week. The whole thing is ridiculous. How would she walk over a thousand kilometres? Where would she get food, shelter and the other things she'd need for a journey like that? What's more, how would I get to Timisoara? How would I send her the 300 marks, even if I had them? I wrote to her and said that the whole thing was stupid. A week later I got a postcard from her accusing me of not being interested in her, and adding that if she were to die tomorrow I wouldn't care.

Dear Adolf, you wrote in your letter that all the papers are ready and now you're only waiting for a visa. If you ask me, I think the next question is what should you do now? Thousands of people get help and this one poor woman isn't getting anything. The Schmulewitsches are partying, getting married in ostentatious weddings, drinking, eating and having a good time. And you Adolf? What are you doing? In spite of the fact that you work hard, you're not prepared to move a finger for Mama.

I feel that I'm at the end of my tether. If something happens to Mama then I'll also die. I want to die. I'm only not doing so now because of three people: you, my dear brother, Judith and Mama.

Here we're at a dead end; at the edge of the world. We're sitting on a volcano. Everything is so expensive, clothing in particular. Only wine is cheap. Judith is growing. Soon she'll be taller than me. I can't buy her any new clothing though. She's brilliant at school and very beautiful. In my next letter I'll send you a picture of her. She looks as if she's fifteen or sixteen, but she's only twelve.

In the autumn Siyoma was taken to a labour camp. We wait in fear that they'll take him again. It could be that the contact between us will break. Please don't waste time – do something. Maybe you should ask the Schmulewitsches to do something? Mama's 59 years old. In Lublin there's cholera and typhus. She wouldn't survive that over there.

Siyoma and Judith send their love.

How are things with you? What's happening with the 'things'? You must make sure that nothing gets stolen. Is Dora married by now? Who to? How's Yette's husband? Is he the German *potz* [penis] that used to come and see her in Leipzig? How was the wedding? I'm really insulted that they didn't invite us. Do you go and see the Schmulewitsches sometimes? What do they say about Mama? You must write to me and tell me everything. I bless you and kiss you from the bottom of my heart. I'd like to bless you with the best of everything and that you'll be successful in all that you do. I hope that we'll see one another soon; they say that by spring the whole thing will be over.

Sei gesund.[6]

Love,
Berta

On New Year's Day, 1940, Lina sent Adolf a telegram, which he received via the Red Cross, in the middle of January.

> The Red Cross
> Citizens Advice Bureau
> Gaddum House
> 16 Queens Street
> Manchester

To: Mr Adolf/Peter Rochman
c/o 55 Clothorne Rd
Manchester 20

> Tuesday, 16 January 1940

---

6. Stay healthy.

Dear Mr Rochman,
We would like to advise you that a telegram has arrived for you from Mrs Lina Rochman in Leipzig. I recommend that you come and pick it up as soon as possible, from our office at the above address.

FROM LINA ROCHMAN
Transmitted through the Red Cross, Saxony.

Leipzig
I January 1940

MY DEAR ADOLF. I AM STILL ALIVE.
I WILL NOT LAST MUCH LONGER. NO FOOD, NO CLOTHING AND NO HEAT.
SAVE ME. MAMA.

Adolf's response:

LINA ROCHMAN C/O LEIPZIG JEWISH COMMITTEE KEILSTR 5.
DEAR MAMA. I AM WELL. GOOD JOB. DOING ALL I CAN TO GET A VISA.
LOVE ADOLF.

On receiving the telegram from his mother, Adolf must have contacted the Schmulewitsches. The next letter is a reply from Zelig Schmulewitsch's son Max (Dora's brother).

Guisborough
Thursday, 18 January 1940

Dear Adolf,
We got your letter today. I've been given the great honour of answering it, as it's usually Dora's job. As for you blaming us for Aunt Lina's situation, you know the political situation very well. I've gone especially to Leeds and had a talk with Graham.[7] He told me that it would be impossible to get your mother into England. The only thing that we can do is to get her into a neutral country; maybe Belgium or Holland. Graham told me he would send you a letter to explain all this.

---

7. The Schmulewitsch's family lawyer.

Do you think that it'll be a problem for her getting from Leipzig to the Belgium border? There must be a train, if not daily, at least weekly. What's the problem? Just getting a ticket and going over there? Why doesn't she do a simple thing like that instead of writing nasty letters to us? I think that the best thing to do is if you take care of all that has to do with the visa (Graham will tell you what to do) and I'll take care of the money side. Now that you have a job, a place to stay and you can speak the language; there's no reason why you can't see to it that she gets a visa.

I understand from Herman that Aunt Lina has had some problems with the police, and will be going to prison; do you know anything about that?

Hope to hear from you soon.

Max

PS. Jane sends her love. She's pregnant, and he will be the first Schmulewitsch to be born in England.

Three weeks after her desperate telegram to Adolf, Lina wrote a long letter to her daughter Berta.

> c/o the Jewish Houses area
> Keilstr. 5
> Leipzig
>
> Sunday, 21 January 1940

My dear Berta,

I got yours and Adolf's letters on the same day. I think Adolf's had arrived a long time ago, but the Gestapo only gave me the two letters together.

I was so worried because I hadn't heard from you for such a long time. Here they say that the Luftwaffe is bombing England every day. I thought that Adolf had been killed. So I was so relieved to get a letter from him. It came through the Red Cross and was only twenty words. He asked if I was well, and I got the Witleses to answer back in 20 words to say that I'm well and that he should tell Aunt that I'm still surviving, but not for long.

From the time that Adolf left, which is now over a year, I think I've got one postcard from her and 200 grams of butter, which the Gestapo or one of those *ganovim* [thieves] in the *kehilla* [community] took half. If you ever write to her, tell her that I really appreciate what she did for me but that it wouldn't kill her to send me some more. I think that living with all her luxuries makes her forget that she has a sister. Tell her that it's fat that I need more than anything else. I don't need her letters telling me how difficult it is in the new country. Maybe send it through the Red Cross. Adolf can't send me any money; anyway there's no use in sending money, as customs or someone over here takes it for the war effort.

I can't stay here much longer; we're all living on the floor of the old sports hall in the Carlebach Schule. Everyday they take people out of here and send them to Poland. Only those who are working stay on. This woman who use to live in Gustav Adolf Str., the one whose husband was the editor of the *Judischers Gemeideblat*, has left for Belgium. Soon I'll be the only Jew left in Leipzig. She's safe now, after her son arranged a visa for her, and you know why? If you don't know I'll tell you – because he cared for her.

I never got an answer from the Swiss Consul, but what Mrs Zellner (who owned the kosher butcher shop in Nordstr.) told me is that you have to go there with a thousand marks as a guarantee. I just don't have this sort of money, and anyway how would I walk all the way to Dresden in my weak condition? On top of that I would need to get a permit from the Gestapo to go there and I'm just too scared to do that.

Tell Adolf that he should go the Swiss consul in England and give in the guarantee money for me there and then send the papers over with the Red Cross, so at least I can get into Switzerland. Tell him that he's forgotten me here and that I'm fading away, with no food to eat, no clothes to wear, no water to drink and no place to live. Tell him to tell Aunt that she should be ashamed of herself. It is a *shande* [shame] what she's doing to me. But Adolf should make sure that he doesn't quarrel with her; she is a sick woman. No, maybe it's better he doesn't say anything to her; she knows she's doing wrong without him telling her.

Dear Berta, you told me that you've started to rent rooms in the house for people coming in from Poland. You mustn't let them take advantage of you. I know how difficult it is when you are all alone.

Dear Berta, you must see that you and Judith never get into a situation like the one I'm in. I should never have believed Adolf; that he'd get me out of here and save me. With all the money you have you must buy shoes; it's so important. If I had better shoes I could walk properly and my feet wouldn't freeze so that now I could have been a free woman. Shoes are the key to your survival. If you don't buy them now you may never know when you'll have the chance to buy them again. Buy with all the money you have because in a short time it'll be worth nothing. Also don't forget to buy boots. If you don't have enough money, take it from your lodgers or from your mother-in-law – they all have money, they're only hiding it. You must also buy fat, petrol, butter, oil, coal and heavy material for clothes. I hope you still have the sewing machine that you took from home.

Dear Berta, you should write to Adolf and ask him to send you the things you can't find – he works in a clothing factory. It's no problem for him to send you buttons, zips, thread – you don't have to be ashamed, everyone does it. It's been a very cold winter here, the coldest I can remember, and not having clothes has made it even harder.

Dear Berta, you must ask Adolf about his illness, how's he managing? Who's doing the cooking for him? You must tell him that he shouldn't eat things with carbohydrates. You must tell him not to forget to do his injection every day.

Dear Berta, tell him not to forget me here. After all, this was his idea; that I should come after he got himself organized. He can't just leave me here. I'll perish away. Don't wait, write right away, now. I'll not live for much longer.

From all our friends there is only Herman Uko and the Zeni family who are still around. I will be the last to leave.

Write to Adolf, and tell him that once he sees to my visa he should see that he gets one for you and Judith. But maybe it's better to stay where you are, now that there's this anti-Semite in England, what's his name – Mos … [Mosley] – something or other, but this Romanian Antonescu fellow in your place isn't much better. I really don't know where we can all go. Maybe the Zionists' idea of living in Palestine is the only solution.

You must write to Adolf and tell him everything that I said. Ask him what's happening with the jewellery? Did the *ganif* [thief] give it back to him?

Stay healthy. I bless you and kiss the child a thousand times. I don't know if I'll ever see her again.

I wish you, Siyoma and Judith a long life, and that dear

God will protect you and Adolf from all evil.

Lots of love from your lonely Mama

Berta forwarded Lina's letter to Adolf.

North Humberland Street
Manchester
28 July 1940

Dear Berta,
I had to cry when I read Mama's letter that you sent on to
me. I feel so helpless in trying to do whatever I can about
getting a visa for her. Uncle David [Oberman] isn't interested and the Schmulewitsches are doing whatever they can
to avoid the subject. Now with the war getting closer, I mean
with the fall of France, no one is interested in anything else.
The big question is, will Britain survive?

Now that we're starting to feel the war more and more,
there's an enormous pressure on us not to be seen in the
streets, not to talk German, to dress like the English, to talk
like the English and to behave like the English. We're also
restricted in our movements; we must report to police once
a day to fill in a form saying where we've been since the last
visit and who we met with. It's starting to be like back home
before I left. Anne's (this English girl I told you about)
brother was with the British Expeditionary Force in France
and was killed last week whilst trying to get on a boat in
Dunkirk. Her parents said that they don't want me to meet
with her anymore because I'm German – as if I had anything
to do with it!

We don't go to the dance halls. We don't go to the cinema.
Thugs, screaming all sorts of anti-Semitic and anti-German
slogans, have attacked the hostel that I'm living in three
times. It's really not the time to go and talk to people about
a visa for Mama. I thought that maybe I should move to
Australia or New Zealand. But now with the Luftwaffe
bombing all day and every day, there're no boats going over
there any more. Even if there were, where would I get the
money for a ticket and visa?

Do you think that it's safe where you are? I guess that
every place is dangerous for the Jews. In the letters I get
from my swimming team friends in Palestine, they say that
in spite of the tension between the Jewish people and the

British it's even worse with the Arabs, but at least there isn't any anti-Semitism. In this little town where they live, which isn't far from Beirut, Hans says that they work very hard and it's very hot, even in the winter. They've organized a defence system and got a van and some rifles from the British Police. Every night they go on patrol to protect the town. He said that some of them have gone on special training missions, to learn guerrilla warfare from some British officer. It seems to me that that is the only place where we can hold our heads up, without having to apologize to anyone for being Jewish. Now I'm really sorry that I didn't go to Palestine with the Bar Kochba swimming team for the Maccabi Games in 1935, and stayed there, like Margolis, Herman and Hecht did. I think that by now I'd have had my own house and I could have brought Mama out there with no problem. But that's crying over spilt milk. I have made a promise to myself though, that if and when I ever get out of this place, and once this war is over, I'll go and live there.

How are things with you? How are things on the farm? Can you still sell the meat and wine? Who's taking care of it when Siyoma goes to the work camps? Here things are bad: they're evacuating children. Most of them are going to the villages around Manchester; some of them even to America. That's also dangerous as most of these boats aren't getting through as they are attacked by the German U-boats.

Do write as soon as you can. We must stay in contact somehow, for as long as it's possible. I'm sure that we'll get Mama out one way or another.

Maybe one day we'll all go to Palestine.

Love,
Adolf

Nearly two months later, Adolf received a reply from his sister.

Cetata Alba
1 October 1940

Dear Adolf,
I'm sorry that it's taken me so long to answer your last letter, but there've been such big upheavals here in the last month that I just didn't get round to it.

From your letter I got the impression that you're not taking care of your health. It seems to me that you're not looking after yourself. Adolf, you must stick to your diet and not eat anything that has any sugar in it. If you don't feel well you must go immediately to the doctor. You mustn't neglect yourself. I think that sometimes you forget that you're alone in a strange country and there's no one there who can look after you.

The other day I got another letter from Mama. Since the Bolsheviks' occupation, letters are just not coming through properly. I'll try to send it on to you. In her letter Mama says that she's completely in despair, she lost her job sorting out the rubbish and therefore is on the list to be deported to the East with the next transport. That was six or seven weeks ago – maybe she's already been sent. There's just no way that I can find out from here.

You wouldn't believe who I met the other day. Do you remember Hans, the son of Franke, the one who had the typewriter shop in Marktstr. – you know the little place on the corner? Maybe you'll remember that he was studying Russian at the time and used to come and practise talking to Siyoma, just after we got married and we were still living with Mama. I was so astonished to see him here with the Red Army that I nearly fell over! Apparently he was deported two years ago, with the rest of the Polish Jews, just before the Brodi synagogue was burned down. As the war started he managed to get to the Russian zone. Now he's an officer with the Red Army, working as a translator. Who would have believed it? He hasn't heard from his parents or brother since he escaped, but he was told that they were in the Lódź ghetto. I asked him if he had seen Mama in one of the places where they bring the stateless Jews from Leipzig. He said that if she was put on one of those cattle trains and transported to Poland, there's no way that she could still be living. He told me that only the young and those who manage to escape survive this week-long journey, with no water, food or sanitation and not being able to sit down the whole way.

I do understand what you said about the visa, but what I don't see is why and where the application is stuck.

I must tell you about these Bolshevik soldiers that came, to 'free' us from Romanian imperialism – calling them animals would be a compliment. From the first day that they arrived the soldiers just went into any house and forced people at gunpoint to bring flowers and to go out to the main street by the castle. Youngsters in police uniforms forced those that had come to the town centre to cheer the troops that had just entered the town. The troops were late as they were busy looting the farmers in Zataka on the way from the river to here. Most of these soldiers come from the inner regions of Russia. They are what we call *muziks*, peasants. The only thing that they know how to do is loot, rape and get drunk.

They are always drunk. Once they found out that we had the wine cellar, they just confiscated it: 'for the war effort' they said. What war are they talking about, they haven't had one day of fighting? The day they came, our 'glorious' Romanian army just ran away, and left us to live with them. They go into houses whenever they feel like it and take whatever they can find. The worst is, if there are young girls or women when they happen to be around, they will just rape them right there and then, and take turns as the others are looting the house. This happened to Larissa's mother and since then she's been ill. She tried to go and complain, and the officer told her that she was a capitalist pig and should know better. She's pregnant now – God knows what will happen.

Ten of them came to live with us. They took over the house and turned it into a brothel, with women coming and going at all hours of the day and night. We had to move into the servant's quarters outside, and we were only allowed into the house to clean up the mess that they made every night. And that's not the worst part of it. When Siyoma showed them his membership card of the Romanian Communist Party, and told them that he had helped working people all his life, the officer told him that he hated communists, saying: 'They took all we had from my family.' He made it clear to Siyoma that if he didn't stop talking about communism and socialism, he would shoot him. One thing that I'm sure of is that German soldiers would never behave in such a way.

We can't go to the beach or the harbour anymore. They've been declared military zones and since then have been completely closed to anyone from the town. We can't even send letters, so I'll have to give this letter to a friend who's going to Jasi and she'll try to send it on from there.

This week I got a letter that made me so angry. It was from Regina's son. You most probably don't know who Regina is. She's Papa's daughter from his first marriage, who left with her mother and brother to go and live in Bonn or Frankfurt after the divorce. I've only met her once when

Papa was on his deathbed – that was before I met Siyoma. I was under the impression that she was only there to see if they were mentioned in Papa's will.

In any case, this letter arrived here about a week ago, from someone I had never heard of before. So he explains who he is, and tells me that he and his parents were deported to Poland since their grandmother (Papa's former wife) came from Warsaw. They are currently living in Suiatyn Staniscawow [Stanislawow], which is in the Russian zone of Galicia. He asked me if I could arrange a visa to get him and his parents into Romania. He also said that a religious man from Manchester took in his sister, Gizla Karpel. He wrote about this man, who'd come across to Germany as a soldier with the British occupational force in 1920 and was invited by his father to religious services during the year or so that he was stationed in Bonn. A short time before they were deported, his father wrote to this person, asking him if he could take his daughter in, so she wouldn't have to go with them to Poland. He agreed, but until all the papers were ready she was in hiding with a German family. Now she's in England and they are in Galicia. Anyway she's working as a housemaid, and doing everything she can to get a visa for him and his parents.

I wrote to her, giving her your address, so if you do get a letter from her, you'll know who she is. What really made me cross about the letter was that not only did he refer to me as 'Liebe Tante Berta', but that he wrote to me in the '*du*' form, as if I'm a friend of his.

Dear Adolf, is there any way that you could arrange for us to get a visa to enter England? Do you think Siyoma could work as an agronomist there? After all that's what he studied and he has a lot of experience, or maybe he could work in an office? He can speak Russian, Romanian, German and even some English.

If there was any way that we could get a visa to Palestine, we would leave tomorrow. I'm sure that he'd find work there in no time; they are looking for people like him, but I think that by now we're too late. It's ironic in a way, when we had the opportunity to go over there and they were prepared to lay down the red carpet for us, we didn't want to go. Now that we're so willing, there's no way to get there.

My mother-in-law is very sick and this thing with the Bolsheviks only makes it worse for her. Once she's gone, they'll take everything away from us. Siyoma told me that in the communist Bolshevik system there's no inheritance and all capitalistic property must be given over to the Party or the state, so we'll all live or die in poverty.

Judith can't go to school as she's the daughter of a capitalist who exploited the workers. It's only 'them' who can send their children to school. It's just such a pity that each day that we stay here feels like a lost day.

The *Tante* from Zurich sent 200 grams of butter to Mama, but Mama, if she's still alive, is so weak and hungry that it won't help her.

I'm working on the farm from morning until night with Siyoma and Judith. We're no longer allowed to employ workers – somehow that's also against the socialist system – but we barely have enough to keep us alive, as we also have to provide for these soldiers that are in the house. About clothes for Judith, there's nothing to say. She's nearly thirteen now and she's growing so fast that the clothes from last year don't fit her any more.

God knows what will happen, I'm afraid that our end may be worse than Regina's.

The only thing that I beg of you, once again, is to do something to save Mama. I don't want anything from you or the Schmulewitsches.

How's Dora? Is she married by now? How do young men and women get together in England? How do they meet?

I love getting your letters. Tell me as much as you can, everything is so interesting.

Siyoma and Judith send their love.

Berta

Inside the envelope there was another letter, from Judith.

Dear Uncle Adolf,
I haven't seen you for such a long time; I can hardly remember what you look like.

My German isn't so good any more so I hope you'll be able to understand what I am writing.

Life isn't as good as it was as we're having a difficult time, but we all hope that it'll get better.

Mama is saying that maybe we'll all come to England, after Oma [Grandma] gets there. Why aren't you helping Oma to come and live with you in England?

I can't play with Larissa anymore, as I'm a capitalist and

she's a worker. When will all this be over?

Love,
Judith

In 1941 Adolf received the following letter from his cousin Max Schmulewitsch, who was interned in a prison camp in Douglas, on the Isle of Man. Adolf too was interned, but as a category D prisoner (despite what Max says), his internment merely restricted him to not being able to leave Manchester.

Dear Peter (just like my sister, I find it difficult to call you Peter),

You lucky bastard. You managed to get out of being arrested in spite of being categorized 'B'. We, I mean all the men in the 'Grey House' fell into category 'C', and we were still sent away. I must admit though that it's actually quite pleasant here. The food's not bad; we're staying in an old resort hotel; the weather is good and we're as far away from the bombing as one can be. So all in all it could be worse. The thing that bothers us most of all is the boredom. There's nothing to do all day long except play chess. I have improved my game threefold, but that's not the reason why we were brought here. We're also forgetting our English.

Our biggest concern is to do with the business, as Herman, Papa and I are here. In the letters we get from time to time from 'the women', it seems that they're coping quite well without us. The main problem, according to Berta, is obtaining raw materials. Every time a ship is sunk by a German submarine there's yet another delay in the yarn arriving in Guisborough. But it seems that they are coping and it's only Papa who thinks that if we, the men, aren't there the factory can't function.

How are things with you? Have you heard anything from Aunt Lina? Some people here have received postcards from members of their families at home: postcards that were sent from work camps in Poland, saying that they're well and are being well treated. They also say they were told that they were brought to these work camps in order to keep them away from the RAF bombings. So if Aunt Lina is sent to one of those work camps, she could have her teeth treated and be given the chance to recuperate.

I do hope that this war will be over soon; it seems to me

that we won't hold out for much longer. Churchill will have to sign a peace treaty.

I hope to hear from you soon and even better, to see you, if we ever get out of this place.

Max

This is one of the last letters from Lina, written on the old wallpaper of the burned-out Brodi synagogue. It is undated.

Dear Adolf,
I am so *varmischt* [confused] that not only do I not know what the date is but I also don't know what day it is. I only know what time it is. I can tell that according to when the guards come and throw food for us over the railing. It's always the young and the strong that get to it first – even before it lands on the floor. I do manage to swipe some morsels off the ground – after each feeding-time. I'm so hungry and thin. I think that I don't weigh much more than 30 kilos. It's funny to think that before this catastrophe, I'd have been so happy if I'd lost some weight.

Dear Adolf, we're living like dogs. No. Worse. At least dogs have a master who'll feed them and take care of them. But we live in the dirt and mud, with no food, water or a place to sleep. I think it's over six or seven months since I've had the opportunity to wash – even in cold water. They say that in a week or two they'll take us to the new territories in the East. There, we are told, we'll get food, clothes and a place to live in – with heating, water and a kitchen. Everyone will have the opportunity to work in their profession. They said that I could work by looking after the children. I must say that I've not worked with children for a long time, but I'm sure that I'll learn very quickly. The only thing that I'm afraid of is that I won't last these next two weeks.

Some people here have received Red Cross postcards from one of the camps in the East, a place called Majdanek or something like that. In the letters they say that the conditions are good and that they are treated well; only that the journey to get there was a bit long. I don't know what I can wear for the train journey; all I have is what I've got on. I wouldn't like to arrive in this new place looking like someone who came out of the poor house. I do hope that they'll give us some new clothes before we leave.

Dear Adolf, you must try and write to me, and send the

letters through Romania or even Russia. You can't leave me and forget me, like all the rest have done.

Don't eat things that aren't good for you. Remember that until I get there, there's no one to take care of you.

I am lonely, hungry and cold.

Love, your Mama

Cetata Alba
Wednesday, 30 April 1941

Dear Adolf,

It took over three months for your letter to arrive. I don't know if this is because of the war or just the inefficiency of the Soviet post system.

I can't remember if I told you in my last letter that Siyoma has been taken, with many other men of his age and younger, into the Red Army. It's now over two months since he was mobilized. We've only received one letter from him. He's stationed somewhere in the Crimean Peninsula, not far from the town of Sebastopol. After Siyoma left, things became worse for us (as if they weren't bad enough before!). At least when he was here he somehow protected me, Judith and my mother-in-law from the Red soldiers. This officer and the group of pigs that have taken over our house have tried once to attack and rape me. Thank goodness Siyoma's brother Miron (he's the one that I told you was the mayor, and the sort of liaison between us and the Russian army in town) just happened to come by with the main officer of the town. He succeeded in bribing them with a pig that he'd brought along. So they left me and went off to slaughter the pig. I'm more worried about Judith and Siyoma's mother and sister than about myself though.

There's a rumour going around, that the German army, after its occupation of Greece and Yugoslavia, will be on its way north to Moldavia. I can only hope that they'll get here soon to free us from Stalin's Red menace. However bad they can be, they can't be worse than these Red pigs who are here now.

Larissa's mother, the one who was raped on the first day these monsters came, had the baby two weeks ago. It's so terrible for her. Not only does she have to care for the child and therefore can't work, but all her friends and relatives are accusing her of having a relationship with the Russians. At least we have some food, either from our farm or from

53

Siyoma's sister's farm, but she doesn't even have that. Our food isn't much and we've finished all the wood we collected for the winter.

Dear Adolf, do you think that there's a way you could get Judith and me into England? The news we get here, which isn't very reliable as it's all from *Izvestia* (the communist newspaper), said that the British imperialist capitalistic army is getting a beating on all fronts and that the Wehrmacht has driven them out of Greece, Yugoslavia and Africa, as well as other places. In England, the newspaper said, things are so bad that everyone is living in bomb shelters and there's no food or fuel. We don't know if any of that is true or not.

Dear Adolf, how are you managing with all this upheaval? Do you have enough to eat? Are you eating the right things? Have you found a woman to marry? What have you done about the visa for Mama? I received a letter from her two or three weeks ago. I'll send it on to you. I've run out of *koyach* [strength]. At least we'll all die together.

Hope you can get a letter to me.

Love,
Berta and Judith

Enclosed was the letter from Lina. It has no date.

Leipzig

Dear Berta,
If no one will save me and get me out today, this will be my last letter. In the meantime they'll come and take me to the new place in the East. They say that I'll have to wait my turn. I think that they take the younger and stronger people first.

We're still rotting here in the old burned-out synagogue. It's getting warmer, thank goodness, so at least we're not freezing at night anymore. But we don't have any water to drink. The only place we can drink is from a broken pipe which drips from the ceiling.

Yesterday my only friend died and her body is still lying around. I only hope that I'll die soon too. If I had had the courage I'd have killed myself long ago. I lost these tablets that I'd bought to do it with and I don't have the courage to do it any other way.

Dear Berta, Adolf has abandoned me and Aunt Sarah has long forgotten that I exist.

Dear Berta, you're the only one that can save me. Don't leave me here.

Your loving Mama

In June 1941 Berta and Judith received a letter from Siyoma, who was stationed in the Crimea.

Lance-Corporal Siyoma Grusman with the
320th Artillery Division
1 June 1941

To my dearest Berta and Judith,
I've been with the Red Army for over three months now. The training is hard and there's a lot of anti-Semitism among the officers. I was recruited to this unit because of my knowledge and understanding of animals. But they have me doing training like all the young soldiers. I have to clean for and serve the officers, as if I was some servant-boy of theirs. I complained to Politroc; I told him that what they're doing is against the first principles of the communist brotherhood. My job should be to take care of the mules. (These beasts were brought here to pull the cannons.) He responded with some very nasty anti-Semitic remark. I must say that I'm very disappointed. I did think that in the army of the working people there wouldn't be any class discrimination. But I see it's no different from any of the capitalistic imperialistic armies anywhere in the world. We get no clothing, no shoes; living conditions are much worse than we gave our farmhands at home. The food is scarce. Our weapons and equipment are old. The officers take all the provisions for themselves when it arrives. Then they give us the leftovers. We Jews in the platoon are always at the end of the queue.

The conditions and training are very poor. I'm only glad that the USSR signed a treaty with Berlin. If the Wehrmacht had launched an attack against us, there wouldn't have been a chance in the world that we could have held the line against them, for even a day.

The soldiers hate the officers; the officers are remorseless in their treatment of the soldiers. And they all hate the revolution and Stalin. Their only dream is to get to America one day. They don't know that in America there is a terrible exploitation of the workers – that doesn't interest them at all.

I miss being at home and most of all I miss you, Judith.

Somehow I think that the whole idea of freedom for the worker – equality for all – isn't getting through to the people.

How are things on the farm? Do the soldiers still live in the house? What happened with the mules? Did the officers give them back as they promised? How is Betya[8] and her family getting on?

The talk is of the British imperial army being in retreat on all fronts. The war will come to an end by the summer and we'll all be able to come home.

I love you both.

Papa

In June 1941 Adolf received the following letter from his cousin Shnoki (daughter of Sarah and Zelig Schmulewitsch) some time after her husband Carol had been released from internment on the Isle of Man.

5 June [1941]

Dear Adolf,

Papa came home last week. He was the last of our family to be released from the camp in Douglas. The factory in Guisborough is working 24 hours a day. It's so busy that we've had to open a new branch in town. Berta and Dora are pulling their hair out trying to find more workers; the problem is getting hold of more male workers. We received an allocation of 50 Italian POWs from the War Office. Most of these workers are from the Italian division in Abyssinia [Ethiopia]. We do have some language problems, but there are three of them who come from the Italian Tyrol and speak some German, with a heavy Austrian accent. Most of them are nice, quiet and hardworking. They work much longer hours than the English. They don't argue, strike or drink. They appreciate anything you give or do for them. Mostly they're glad to be away from the war front. The War Office takes care of them – food, lodgings and a monthly visit by the Red Cross, and even gives them some pocket money. At every shift they arrive, chained to one another, escorted by a military policeman, although I don't think that they're trying to escape, but who knows? Some of the girls on the

---

8. Siyoma's sister, who also owned a farm in Cetata Alba.

factory floor have cast an eye on one or two of them. (Most of them are no older than twenty-three.) The truth is, I can't blame them. I'd do the same if I wasn't married. There are three of them who come from Milan. Before the war they worked as cutters, which is a great help to us. One of them is so good that he saves us some 50 yards of material a week, most of it from the officers' uniform allocation fabric that we get from the Board of Trade. With what he saves, we make civilian clothing. Herman takes it down to London each time he goes. He sells it to clothing stores down the 'Lane'.

The bombing has stopped. It's only the black-outs, the rationing, the lack of men in the street and an occasional air raid siren that remind you that we're still at war.

With me going on about the Italians, I forgot to tell you that Dora is getting married and Jane is pregnant. Do you remember the boy that you brought with you, before they all left for Douglas? Well, Papa, Herman and Max were interned with him. When they were released he came to work with us, or should I say with them, as I'm still in Hartlepool.

I miss not being with the family in the Grey House. Carol and Lotti aren't nice to me. If I look back, Papa was right opposing my marriage to Carol. I think that he and Lotti just see me as someone who can hold the shop for them when they're away. I know that when Carol goes away, or when he goes on his civil patrol duty, he sees other women.

From the bits and pieces of news that we get from home, things seem to be very bad. They're sending more and more Jews to the East. From time to time people get postcards here from relatives in the work camps. In the postcards they say that they are well and things are good, but I don't believe it.

A few days ago, I read an article by some Polish Jew, in the *Hartlepool Gazette*. The article said that he'd escaped from one of those camps in the East. He told the reporter that they aren't work camps, as they are portrayed as being, but that they're slaughterhouses for Jews and gypsies; places where the Germans get rid of people they don't know what to do with. But who knows what the truth is? To me, it seems somewhat exaggerated that they'd slaughter people like animals.

Thank goodness winter's over. Do you know that I nearly finished all the wood I bought before the winter? Now with all these ships being sunk by the German U-boats, there isn't enough heating fuel. I've been thinking of Aunt Lina and what's happening to her. Maybe it's better if she is taken to the East. She could wait there until the end of the war. Even if it is true that they sometimes shoot people there, I'm sure that they wouldn't do that to a harmless old lady like your mother.

I hope to hear from you soon. Don't be lazy and write soon. Mama hasn't heard from you since they came back from Douglas.

All my love,
Shnoki

In 1941 Adolf received another letter from his friend Arnold, now a bus driver in Palestine.

Nahariya
Palestine
[1941]

Dear Adolf,
I met Hans the other day in the street. He was on leave from the western desert. He told me that he'd received a letter from you and gave me your address. I was really sorry to hear what's going on with your mother.

I don't know if he told you, that Ayala (from the swimming team; maybe you remember her as Gizella?) and I got married. (Just a reminder – it was you who introduced us.) By doing so it was easier to get a visa for me. You may remember that we stayed after the Maccabi Games in 1935, but she had a visa and I didn't.

We live in Nahariya; the same town as Hans. Like Hans, I started off with a rooster farm, but then Ayala's brother got out and came to live with us in Palestine. He managed to smuggle out some money and with it we bought shares together in a bus cooperative. It's over a year now that we've been working together as bus drivers and I just love it. Back at home we would have never dreamed of doing something like this, but here it's different. Here in the *Yishuv* it's considered highly respectable work. Each member must put the price of half a bus into the cooperative and once you have done that you're a member/partner for life. Gidalia (my brother-in-law) and I are working on the same share for the time being. (I think you know him too; he used to be in the reserve team for the water polo.) My job is to drive our bus once a day to Haifa and back, and once a week to Beirut.

Most of what we do is drive around the Middle East, transporting soldiers of the Eighth Army. So I get to go to all those remote places that as children we always dreamed about. Places like Baghdad, Damascus, Teheran, Baalbek, Jerusalem and Cairo.

In the last month or so there's been a war in Syria. The war was between the British Eighth Army and the French (those loyal to Vichy France). I know that there were some other French troops that were part of the Free French Army, supporting someone called General de Gaulle. The whole thing is too complicated for me to understand; I can't figure out who is loyal to whom, and who is with the Eighth Army and who are agents. So how do I know about all this? About a month ago, we started transporting big numbers of the Eighth Army troops north, towards Damascus. On the way back we took French and German POWs to the prison in Acco. On one of these journeys, coming back from Damascus two weeks ago, I heard one of the prisoners talking to his friend in a very clear Saxon accent. At one of the stops the Australian officer on guard allowed me to go and talk to him. I found out that his parents apparently live in Meneknstr. in Leipzig. I remember visiting your cousin on the same street. Isn't it by the lake? He told me that he's been in the army for the last six months as a wireless operator. Until the time he was sent to Syria, he was stationed in Leipzig and could go home frequently. When I asked him what was happening to the Jews, he said that there are very few Jews left in Leipzig. Those who are still living in the city congregate round or in the old Brodi synagogue. The few that are seen walking around the town look as if they were pulled out of the sewer canals. They are dirty, scruffy and hungry-looking. Their clothes look as if they haven't been changed for months. On top of that he said they smelt as if they hadn't washed or shaved for months. This, he said, surprised him. He remembered his Jewish friends and neighbours in Golis always being dressed in the best clothing and looking spik and span. He couldn't understand what had happened to them in the last year. His father, who works as a clerk for the Gestapo administration, told him that there were only a few Jews left in Leipzig. He said that in a short time they would all be sent to work camps in the East. He didn't like the army and was glad to be out of the battlefront. He was worried that his parents wouldn't know where he was. He thought he could send them a message through the Red Cross. This Leipzig boy was told by his superiors that it's only a matter of months before the British forces all over the world just collapse and surrender. That will be the end of the war, he was told. Russia won't last more than two months. Their information officers told them that by Christmas all the boys would be home. So he thinks that being a POW until then is better than soldiering.

Considering how things seem from here, i.e. with the British imperial troops in retreat on all fronts, who knows, he could be right?

Hans told me that you've had big problems getting your mother out. I hope that by now it has been sorted out.

Here in Palestine it's very hot everywhere you go. We only have rain two or three months of the year, so we can swim in the sea, which is just down the road, all the year round. It's funny to see the local Arab people come out and dance when the first rains start in October or November.

In the few years that I've been here I've managed to learn Arabic and some Hebrew, which is the modern biblical language. The Hebrew isn't difficult, if you know some of the Jewish prayers we learned in school. But I just can't master English. It takes me such a long time to find the right word in English for what the POW is saying in German. I really hope that by the time the war ends I'll know more just because of doing some translating.

This town that we live in is about halfway between Beirut and Haifa.

I'm only sorry that you're not here. We miss your training. I'm sure that you would have improved your swimming tenfold.

We both miss you.

Arnold

The following letter was written by Marissa, Siyoma's brother's wife, to Adolf. Miron, Siyoma's brother, had converted to Christianity many years before, and as Marissa was not Jewish she was in no danger of being arrested, detained or deported.

Marissa was an illiterate Romanian peasant woman. The letter was written in Russian, with the help of a neighbour. It describes the terrible fate of Adolf's sister and niece, Berta and Judith, at the hands of the Romanian Green Shirts (a paramilitary fascist organization) in August 1941.

The letter never reached its destination. It was returned after Glasnost in 1990 to Marissa.

Thursday, 15 August 1941

Dear Mr Adolf Rochman,

I'm writing this letter with my neighbour's help. He doesn't know German but I hope that you'll find someone who can translate this letter for you. Miron is not here.

My name is Marissa. I am Miron's wife. I found your address among the scattered papers that were left behind by your sister. She had lived in the servant's quarters on their farm since the Russian occupation last year.

The Germans, who came into our area about two months ago, chased the Red Army out. Berta, who was always so pragmatic, didn't escape across the Dniester along with the rest of the Jews. She thought that the Germans would be looking for people like her: people with whom they had a shared language and culture. She thought that someone like her could help communicate with the local population. The plunderings, lootings and raping that followed the communist occupation had stopped for some time. The Germans seemed to be in control and things returned to some sort of normality.

Berta decided to go to the Castle. She planned to work for them as a nurse, secretary or translator. After being there for a while she thought that she would go to the Commandant. Berta knew that if she told him what the Bolsheviks had done to them and to the other German families, the Commandant would give an order that would see to it that she and her family would get back all of their property that had been confiscated from them. I told her not to go: 'Let sleeping dogs lie', I said. Fortunately, at the gate she met this soldier that she knew. Apparently he had been a student of hers in the Leipzig Musical Institute. He told her not to dare to go in, 'That will be the end for you and Judith', he said. He told her that she should go into hiding right away. Through his connections with the secretarial staff of the Commandant he said that he would see if he could get her a permit to cross the river. In the meantime she should do all she could to obtain a certificate as a Romanian peasant. As a Romanian she could then claim that her husband and farm was across the river. Until then she needed to stay out of sight. He would also do all he could to bribe the Romanian Legionnaires Police search parties. Hopefully he would be able to keep them away from the farm. He made it clear that time was short. He knew of German plans to liquidate all the Jews and communists in the town.

Berta then went home, picked up Judith and came to our place. She was in complete shock. I had never seen her in such a state. We couldn't keep them here though. Informers are everywhere – it could have been very dangerous. So, at night the three of us sneaked into the wine cellar on their farm. By moving bottles we managed to create a small hiding niche for them behind the wine vat. At night, I would come with food and leave it at the old stable. Later one of them would come out and take it.

Berta's student from the Musical College kept his promise. The search parties visited all the houses where there was suspicion that Jews or communists may have been hiding but they never came to Trayan 50. I knew this, as we live just across the street from their farm.

For a time the Wehrmacht and the Romanian army stopped all other activity. People in the market said that they were preparing for a war against the Soviets. During this time, I tried to get the Romanian forged papers, but it wasn't possible. No one would help me and I can't read or write. I didn't have the money the forgers wanted for the counterfeit papers.

About a month ago, Berta's former student had moved on with the German army into Russia. There was no one left who could protect them.

Then one morning, two or three weeks ago, from my window I saw the Green Shirts entering the farm. They went straight to the wine cellar. They had an informer with them. There was absolutely nothing I could do to stop them. I went out into the street and joined the other neighbours outside the house.

The Legionnaires came out with a soldier dragging the two of them across the yard. They pulled Berta by her hair but although she was being dragged backwards, Berta tried to pick herself up. Each time she did so, one of the Garda de Fier thugs would clobber her with his baton. This whole thing only took a few moments, but to me it seemed like an eternity. Once they got to the lorry that was waiting on the street, they just threw the two of them in. Other Jews and Bolshevik supporters were already inside the van. Then they drove off. Our eyes met for a second, but I dropped my face immediately. I was afraid that one of the Legionnaires would suspect that I was associated with them. Since then I can't sleep at night. I feel like Peter when he betrayed our Lord.

They were driven to the old synagogue. There the Romanian police gathered all the Jews that they had arrested. I don't know what has happened to them since then.

I walk by there nearly every day. I'm hoping to see one of them from the windows or in the courtyard. Each time somebody does come close the Garda de Fier just chases them away.

Today I overheard in the market that each night the guards take groups of them out to the forest and shoot them. I just don't know whether that's true or not.

The Germans and Antonescu's people take food from us. We're only allowed to have one loaf of bread in the house. They even take the food that we grow in the garden. If anyone is caught smuggling food, he's taken to the Castle. Most people don't come back from there. They say that they take them to work in Germany.

I don't know how long we will last. No one has any idea how long they'll stay alive in the synagogue, with no food or water.

I don't know if you'll receive this letter, but I'm sending it through people who can get this sort of letter through. Please don't answer me. It's dangerous to receive letters and in any case I can't read.

Marissa

The following letter was written by Siyoma on a military postcard only allowing 22 lines. Siyoma was unaware that his wife and daughter had been killed.

From Sergeant Siyoma Grusman
56th Army 320th Infantry Division
15 September 1941

My dearest Berta and Judith,
It's over a month since I've heard from you. I do hope all is going well. We have been fighting against the German army for the last month in the city of Kerch. Many soldiers have

been killed. We don't know what will happen. We're on the move all the time, so there's not much time to write.

Write as soon as you can.

Your loving father,
Siyoma

Siyoma ended up in Tashkent in Mongolia. This was the last letter he wrote to Berta and Judith. He was killed in the battle of Kerch in eastern Crimea in October 1941.

When Adolf wrote the following letter in September 1941, he did not know that his sister and niece were dead.

Manchester
Sunday, 21 September 1941

Dear Berta,

It's some time since I've heard from you. I've also not heard anything from Mama. I can only hope that you and she are still well and that the war hasn't interrupted your life too much. The last letter I received from you, in which you told me about the Red soldiers and how they were treating you, was over six months ago. Now that the Germans are there it must be better, at least for you.

I just must tell you my big news.

On Yom Kippur, not only did I decide to fast but also to go to *shul* [synagogue]. As I'm not a member of any particular synagogue, I choose to go to the Romanian *shul* in Cheetham Hill Road. I hoped to meet someone that had recently come over from there. A person who could perhaps shed some light on what's happened to you and Judith in Cetata Alba. I didn't meet anyone who even knew where Cetata Alba was, let alone anyone who'd met you or Siyoma. But I did meet this small manufacturer, who's a producer of bolts and nuts for the Ministry of War. He offered me a job in this four-man factory of his, where I started to work just after Kol Nidre. He also arranged for me to rent a room in one of the bedsits that they have. The other day his daughter came home on leave from the army. Her beauty stunned me – a sort of healthy look that one doesn't see in Jewish women. The women's RAF uniform that she was wearing made her look even more attractive. She looks so much like her father – tall, slim, with a kind-looking face. Her job is to drive a lorry loaded with aeroplane parts. Everyone calls her

Mike, but her real name is Myrtle. Her father and mother are cousins and they're both second-generation Romanians. The two families came from Maichan in central Romania. When I looked it up on the map I saw that it's by 'Gals'. It looked about halfway between your town and Bucharest. I wonder if you know it. One thing led to another, and we started to go out together each time she had leave from the Air Force. Mostly we've been out to dance halls. Now it seems to be much more serious than any other relationship that I've had before. The funny thing is that until she she joined the WRAF she was a member of the British Communist Party – just like Siyoma was when you met him.

I'm going to send a telegram to Mama via the Red Cross with the news.

I hope that you'll receive this letter, in spite of the war.

Love,
Adolf

In October 1941 Adolf received a letter from Fritz Bloedel, a family acquaintance from Leipzig (living in the United States). Fritz had news of Lina.

Des Moines
Iowa
15 October 1941

Dear Mr Adolf Rochman,
You most probably don't remember me. I'm Max Bloedel's son; he had the auto repair shop on Bornaische Str. I'm sure you won't know me because I didn't go to the Carlebach Schule.

As my mother isn't Jewish (I was considered a *Mischlinge* [person of mixed race]), we could have got a permit to leave, but to do that she was told that she needed to denounce her marriage to my father. This involved admitting in front of a judge that she'd made a mistake by marrying a Jew; admitting to *Rassenschande*. She could have done it when my father was deported with the Polish Jews but she didn't want to. She thought it would be too shameful. So we had to stay with the rest of the Jews in the burned-out synagogue. About two months ago, just before the Russian campaign, they transferred us all to the former cellar of the Lübecker synagogue in Gustav Adolf Str. There were over 400 people shoved into this hole in the ground. We had no protection from the rain or the sun: men, women and children all together. Above us were guard-posts and the SS looked down at us from the top. From time to time they took people away to work camps in the East.

This was just too much for my mother. So eventually she gave in and a short time later we got a permit to come to New York, where my aunt lives. From there I was sent to boarding school in Des Moines, Iowa.

Your mother gave me your address and asked if I would contact you somehow when I got to freedom. She looked bad – like all of us. I don't see how she'll last. She was hoping that she'd be sent to the work camps in the East. She thought that there she'd get better food and conditions. I think that was her only hope that was keeping her alive. We all lived with this hope. Now I know that anyone sent there is killed and burned. She has no clothes, no food and no place to sleep. Just before we left, the Committee took all the blankets from us. They told us that it was 'for the war effort'. She can only get food once a day, from what's left on the floor after the guards throw bread from the top. That's not enough to live on.

I don't want to tell you how and what you should do – I'm sure that you're doing the best you can to get her out. But I would like to make the point that if she's not released shortly, it could be the end of her. Either she'll be sent to the East or just die from hunger, exposure or exhaustion. I'm astonished that she has held out for so long. I don't know what to advise you. I hope you'll find a way.

Fritz

In November 1941 Adolf wrote the following telegram (in German) to his mother. He sent it through the Red Cross.

Friday, 14 November 1941

DEAR MAMA
I HAVE FOUND A GIRL TO MARRY, FROM A GOOD ENGLISH FAMILY. ALL IS WELL WITH ME.
ADOLF.

Some time later, he received the following reply from Lina:

Thursday, 20 November 1941

DEAR ADOLF
WONDERFUL NEWS. MAY YOU HAVE A LONG LIFE. I
WILL BE SENT OVER TO THE EAST IN A WEEK OR TWO.
WE WILL MEET AFTER THE WAR. I AM HUNGRY.
MAMA.

Shortly afterwards, he received the following momentous news from the British immigration authorities.

Friday, 21 November 1941

Dear Mr Adolf Rochman,
I am glad to inform you that the entry visa you applied for in the name of Mrs Lina Rochman from Leipzig, Germany has been granted. You are kindly requested to come to our office on 97 Kings Road to see to the formalities.

Herbert Morrison
Undersecretary for Immigration

But by the time this news reached Adolf, it was already too late. At the end of November 1941, Lina, with the rest of the Jewish prisoners, was taken from the former cellar of the Lübecker synagogue in Gustav Adolf Strasse to the central prison in Leipzig. Adolf received this message, written on a Red Cross postcard, from her:

15 January 1942

Dear Adolf,
I'm feeling a bit better, the food is good here and they are treating us well.
They promised that in a week or two we'll be sent to family work camps in the East, where things will be much better. They told us that they're doing this so that we won't have to suffer from the food shortages and be exposed to the British air bombings.
Dear Adolf, can you send me 60 marks through the Red Cross so I can pay for the train?

We'll meet after the war. I'll send you my new address once I get there, so that you'll be able to find me. They say that by Christmas it will all be over.

Your loving Mama

In 1942 a Red Cross enquiry about Lina Rochman drew the following reply, which was translated from a Gestapo document.

6 FEBRUARY 1942

WHEREABOUTS OF LINA ROCHMAN
SEPTEMBER 24 MOVED FROM HER RESIDENCE IN KEIL STRASSE 5 FIRST FLOOR TO THE LÜBECKER SYNAGOGUE GUSTAV ADOLF STRASSE BOTTOM FLOOR. LEFT FOR AN UNKNOWN DESTINATION 30 NOVEMBER 1941.
WAS LAST SEEN ON THE TRAIN LEAVING FOR RIGA IN THE NEW TERRITORIES ON 5 FEBRUARY 1942.

On Lina's train journey to Riga there was a woman who had taught at the Carlebach Schule in Leipzig. This woman, Helga, survived the Holocaust and now lives in Israel. It was through her that the family later learned that Lina had died on the train. On arrival at the railway station in Riga, her body was taken and later burned in the crematorium in the main camp.

Part 2
STORIES

The Boarding House

LILY WAGNER

I found this story when I was researching for material in the Wiener Library in London. It appeared to encapsulate much of the refugee experience of the time.

Dr Lily Wagner left Berlin and came to London in 1938. It soon became evident that it would be impossible for her to pursue her writing career (she specialized in writing articles on the natural and behavioural sciences) to keep herself and her children. According to her daughter, Irene Bloomfield, she was 'a superb homemaker and always knew what would look right and be comfortable, so she decided to give a home to the many other refugees who had lost their own'. It is their stories that she tells in 'The Boarding House', also known as 'Emigrants' Daily Life'.

Dr Wagner died in 1967.

No one could call it a promising start. I had exactly 16 shillings in my pocket and London to woo. Sixteen shillings between the past and the conquest of the future.

At first there was no need to worry about food and shelter. A former colleague of mine, with whom I had worked for some time, had offered me hospitality for the first weeks. I had entered the country with a working permit as a freelance journalist, so there was at least some basis to rebuild my broken career. But I was not alone; with me was my younger daughter, Inge, then 16 years old, whom I desperately wanted to save from becoming a domestic servant; this being the hard lot of almost every refugee girl including my elder daughter. She too had entered the country with a domestic permit and had been working for more than a year in a saloon bar.

Our initial home with a friend seemed like a symbol of the immigration: the combination of tiny kitchen and bathroom

71

where butter and jam-pots peacefully shared the same shelf with toothbrush and glass. This little room had brought it home to me that we all had to renounce, quite consciously, our former mode of living: all our small comforts and luxuries. A new life had to be begun – a hard life without snugness and bourgeois respectability.

I had come to London on 2 February 1938. On 13 March the balloon went up, so to speak, and it was announced that Hitler had annexed Austria. Each day we had more alarming news. One horror followed another.

I decided that I had to find work that was more closely connected with my new life. Above all, I felt I must try to help the refugees who arrived here homeless and desperate. Was there a possibility of opening a home for them? Of giving them an atmosphere that would make them forget their misery, their sufferings, if only for a time? I thought about using my furniture, which was in storage, for a home for refugees – those immigrants who had lost everything in one single blow. A home offering an intellectual and social centre where they would not feel lonely and where companionship with peoples from the same country would be a consolation; where their personal fate and suffering could be borne more easily because it had become the fate of them all.

It was by a stroke of chance that I met a charming young English woman, Mrs Juliette Wilson, who also felt very strongly about the position of these immigrants, and who, like myself, was filled with the desire to help them in whatever way possible. We agreed that the rooms should be warm and cosy, and that there should be a kind and understanding hostess to mother them and to help them to overcome their temporary depression. Many of them had no knowledge of the English language and were far too nervous and absorbed in their fate to be able to make the slightest effort at learning. First of all they needed to be able to collect their thoughts and to discuss their problems in their own language, before they were strong enough to concentrate on even the lightest mental work. Older people, who could not get used to the strange English surroundings, were terribly unhappy and cried their eyes out, sometimes for days, because they could not understand anything except

72

'yes', 'no' or 'isn't it a lovely day?' They did not understand the English mentality, and could hardly be expected to do so.

Mrs Wilson promised her full cooperation on condition that we should place all our available furniture at her disposal and contribute what help we could from our intimate knowledge of continental people and customs. The house needed to be opened as soon as possible; for our part, we also needed a niche where we could sleep. She wanted no profit from the venture, just the satisfaction that the very best had been done with the limited means available. The idea was hospitality, not financial gain.

Mrs Wilson's condition that we were to find a suitable house and furnish it was no easy task, as she herself possessed just as little money as we did, and could supply nothing but high ideals and goodwill.

Puck, my elder daughter (still known by that very apt child-hood nickname of hers), also came into our ranks, and goodwill became the order of the day. She had given up her former job and she and her sister lived with some relatives of mine. We undertook to seek a suitable place and we trudged about in London's streets, sometimes very wearily, to look for the house of our dreams.

We saw many houses, chiefly in Hampstead, where most of the German immigrants had settled. Eventually Puck found it – the house of our dreams, the house that was to become our fate, our life.

To me it seemed madness even to think of it as a possibility. It was in one of the very nicest districts, in the nicest street of the borough. The agent had given us the address and had made an appointment with the landlady. I hardly dared to venture into this elegant mansion, but Puck resolutely rang the bell and showed the maid the agent's letter. We were taken to a beautiful sitting room and received by a smart and pretty Englishwoman: a real lady. After asking numerous questions about our scheme, she gave us a kind welcome, offering us tea and a lovely home-made cake, which increased our courage and warmed our hearts. We told her everything about our plans and hopes, and also the regrettable scantiness of our means.

The lady smiled, obviously aware of the strange difference in her position and ours. She belonged to one of the most respected nations in the world; she was a rich woman, living in her own house, her own country, and had little to fear regarding her future. We must have seemed like gypsies, nomads in search of a safe resting place.

If Mrs Challen mistrusted us and our enterprising spirit she did not let us notice it. Here Puck's knowledge of English, gleaned during her year in the saloon bar, was invaluable. We would have been helpless without her as our interpreter.

Mrs Challen seemed to consider the proposition seriously, but she had to consult with Mr Challen. Eventually a few days later Mr Challen informed us that he had decided to let us have the house, although we did not possess a bank account. I had not realized how unusual a procedure that was, until the house agent told us that he had warned Mr Challen not to accept us as tenants after he had found out about the missing bank reference.

So our venture had begun, but it proved to be no bed of roses. The expenses of running a household, however economically, are not trivial at any time. But at the end of April we were installed in the most comfortable house in Hampstead, with a balance of ten shillings in hand. What speculation this must seem to people who have never tasted the bitterness of persecution, such as we had known. But in our tragic situation, as refugees and Jews, what was there left for us but a sporting chance? It was not our real nature to scamper about on the edge of a financial precipice. We longed for a settled existence, for recognition of our rights as human beings. It is so difficult for happy, settled people to understand the feelings of those who have lost their way. If our British friends and benefactors judged us, they should never forget that we could not act naturally and do as we should have liked and, moreover, as they would have wanted and expected us to do.

Consider, for instance, the fate of those older ones among the refugees; those who had careers in medicine, law and commerce and now had no more hopes of working. Many of them had suffered for months in concentration camps before their release from their native country. Humiliation and illness in the face of old age swept away their zest for living; in many cases their very desire to live. Can you blame them, if they did not find the right way, if they made mistakes and tried the impossible?

But I fear I am digressing on the emotional side, while the adventure waits to be unfolded.

At last we were installed in our castle, as I liked to call the beautiful house, and were expecting our first guest, a young Viennese lady whom I had met years ago. When Austria was annexed by the Nazis, her father, the owner of a well-known fashion house, had committed suicide. Her brothers, of whom she had no news whatsoever, had been imprisoned in Dachau. She was a wealthy, good-looking woman, with a wonderful voice. Often she had been asked to sing in the Viennese broadcasting house. Now this woman, who had always moved in the best circles in Viennese society, had come from Austria, together with her fiancé, a young doctor, who had been forced to give up a most promising career as a specialist for nervous diseases. Both arrived here without a penny. Fortunately a former girlfriend who had become a naturalized British subject had deposited a considerable sum of money at Lloyd's Bank in their favour, so that they could make a good start without any direct worries. When I met her again by accident at Woburn House, the original centre of the Refugee Aid Committee, she was still full of hope, expecting to get permission to work as a singer. (This was later refused.) She happened to tell me that they were looking for a nice inexpensive boarding house, in which to live, as they could not afford to stay much longer at their Kensington hotel. The way seemed to be opening up for our project. With great glee we invited them to come and view our house, which they did that same evening. They decided to take two rooms on the top floor, where the windows overlooked the nearby little park.

As we had no money left – not even to buy food with – I had to go and see them at their hotel in Kensington and ask them to pay the first few weeks' rent in advance. It was a difficult step for me to take, and our guests, having been accustomed to every comfort and luxury in the past, were obviously taken aback by my strange request. It was a little ironic that even some of our own people, refugees like ourselves, found it difficult to understand how we could be in occupation of such a house and yet in such urgent need of money. Nor had they yet realized that they would soon have to face life's problems and work in strange jobs. Still, I did not have to say much, and she handed me an oblong piece of white paper printed with old English lettering and script. Without demur I accepted what appeared to me to be a cheque; but it turned out to be a five-pound note – my first – which I proudly showed to my daughters.

So we were able to fill the larder and rest assured that for at least three weeks we were able to live a normal working life. My daughter Puck was a wonderful help to us. Her year of domestic training had taught her the essentials of household management, and she could now apply with pleasure what she had learned with sadness. Also my younger daughter, proud that she had been educated in a modern Swedish boarding school where the curriculum included domestic science, was happy to have the chance to prove the value of her studies and helped enthusiastically.

In the meantime, a limited company had been formed, as our work grew to such an extent as to necessitate a business organization. Mrs Wilson, whom we respected as director of our affairs, gave her services in the most unselfish manner and contributed immeasurably to the happiness and well-being of the refugees. Some time previously she had served on one of the most important committees at Woburn House, and later at Bloomsbury House, where all the refugees in London were registered. The organization and the work of Bloomsbury House is unique and remarkable. Its numerous departments dealt with every problem which might confront a refugee. Thousands of people who entered this country quite destitute were supported for many months, and in some cases for years, by the Aid Committee. Work permits were not easy to obtain in view of the unemployment problem already existing in England. The refugees will always be grateful to the people of this country for the very humane way in which they endeavoured to cushion the effects of one of the greatest racial upheavals in history. It is true that in every department of life there will be individuals who can find something to complain about, but with the refugees such cases were few and the complaints founded on insufficient training in the school of life. The Refugee Aid Committee can never be praised enough.

Through the aid of the committee our house was soon filled

with guests who were thankful to find a good home at little cost, and we soon had so many applications that we were able to open a second and even a third and fourth home. It would have been a most interesting experience for any keen student of human nature to have lived in our house during these two years, after the annexation of Austria, when there was such a great influx into London of all sorts of people. One could not but feel apprehensive as to how all those people were going to carve out their separate futures in their new country.

The position of these newcomers was different from that of some of the earlier refugees who had emigrated several years before them. These earlier immigrants, mostly professional people, had come over one by one, obtained their work permits and continued in their own professions, mostly as doctors, dentists, etc., much as they had done in Germany. Others, who had a bit of money, opened factories or business establishments and worked in cooperation with English business people. Most of them, having begun to learn English on their arrival, had a fair command of the language, and they had the advantage of having been able to bring their worldly goods with them. It was simply a change of domicile for them, and was not accompanied by the suffering experienced by later refugees. These people never really knew what immigration meant. After a comparatively short time they were fully established in their new homes, with their own furniture, surrounded by their old books and pictures. They had come from Berlin or Frankfurt to London, just as might have happened under ordinary circumstances. Through their work they soon made contact with English people, and with the help of their colleagues they were able to settle down and fit in with their new surroundings easily and comfortably.

How vastly different was the mass immigration during the last two years for the Austrians after the annexation of their country and the Germans after the November persecution! Without any warning, without any preparation, the unfortunate Viennese Jews were thrown out of their splendid villas and hunted out of the country. Whereas the German Jews had had the chance to resign themselves to the changed circumstances and to get used to the years of increasing difficulties and insults that they had to encounter, the change in Austria had been too rapid to be fully understood. There people had neither the chance nor the time to absorb what was happening. After some nightmarish weeks in Vienna, or in Dachau, they arrived in England, without any fundamental change in their outlooks. They had not had long enough to forget the advantages of their former lives. They could not forget spring in Vienna, nor the Walses or the Vienna woods. They talked incessantly about the better cooking, the more comfortable rooms, the better heating system in Austria, and complained about everything. They told everybody about their magnificent houses, their high-powered cars and their servants. They constantly compared their present miserable life to the paradise they had lost.

And yet, paradoxically, those who were actually used to this life of luxury were more ready to forget what had been and more willing to do any sort of work, given a permit. Owners of big stores served stoically as butlers and parlour maids. A former MP tried to sell continental delicacies. Famous writers and scientists lived by copying circulars and addressing envelopes.

It was far worse for the lower classes, the 'nobodies'. Those people who used to live in the backyards of the beautiful Viennese houses trying to exist on a very small monthly allowance, and sometimes not even sure of that. The pensioners and commercial travellers, who with trade stagnant had lived in penury, lost all sense of proportion. They thought that all being immigrants, all were equal. Living here in a strange country it did not matter what one was before. In their fantasies their little flat in the slums had grown into a suite of rooms filled with luxury; their charwoman became a staff of servants; the weekly visit to the local cinema became a box in the opera house. Bank clerks, to whom fate had denied success, told us all about the marvellous life they used to lead as bankers of infinite importance and influence, and people who perhaps once in their lives had made an insignificant contribution to a minor newspaper led themselves to believe in their vocation as famous writers. The longer that they were away from home the more they came to believe their stories and take their pathetic fantasies for reality. The real 'somebodies' tried to forget their former lives as rapidly as possible.

These people from humble backgrounds were sure to get the best of everything. They demanded and expected the most extravagant things and were neither willing nor able to adapt themselves to their new surroundings. Their children were spoilt, noisy, showy and intensely badly brought up. (Though I must admit that amongst the children of the educated people there were also regrettable examples of ill-breeding.) Comparison with the well-behaved English children, brought up either at home or in the strict discipline of the public schools, was not at all in their favour. It seemed that we could learn quite a lot from our hosts.

There were for instance Hänschen and Fritzchen, to me the most outstanding specimens of ill-bred children. One lovely summer's evening I was relaxing in a deck-chair in the garden after a hard day's work, when all of a sudden two gentlemen called and insisted on an interview with me. One of them, with astonishing eloquence and persistence, tried to point out to me that I simply had to admit his wife and small children. He had tried all day to find rooms for them, but had always been refused on account of the children. His wife was terribly run down and quite unable to stand any more worries. She was in a state of distress, quite likely to commit suicide under the prevailing nervous strain. The man seemed to be exhausted and kept assuring me that he had been promised by the Committee to be admitted and repeatedly stressed we would not be allowed to reject him.

Mrs Wilson and I talked things over and finally we could not bring ourselves to send him away without a satisfactory answer. What we had always wanted to do was to give help where help was most needed. Of course the answer was a favourable one, and it was arranged that his wife and children would come the following day. He did not fail to assure us how very well-behaved his children were, and we were glad to hear that they would be no trouble whatsoever.

Well, Hänschen and Fritzchen, when they did appear, turned out to be little devils personified. Nobody, not even their over-indulgent parents, could possibly have been serious in finding them charming. They did everything to shatter the well-balanced everyday routine of the boarding house. They shrieked constantly at the top of their voices for no conceivable reason – they simply loved noise for its own sake. When at large in the park, they quarrelled and fought with the English children and quite definitely enjoyed being as naughty as possible. Their favourite occupation in the morning was to run around in the dining room soiling the dainty pink brocade of the chairs with bread and jam on their dirty, sticky paws. It was hopeless to expect their parents' assistance, for they never found fault with them.

Spoiled brocade covers, broken chairs, burned tablecloths, smashed furniture and china – damage done by the carelessness and thoughtlessness of the refugees – I learnt to take it all stoically. After all, what did a few yards of brocade matter to us, those who had lost all we were so closely tied to: the Fatherland, the German woods, the men and women who used to be our friends and comrades, who had, like us, believed in freedom and brotherhood, in science and progress? What became of them? They did irreparable evil. And should we have worried about a yard of pink brocade!

Pipifax was another disgusting example of this type of ill-bred child. Her parents, a doctor from Cologne and his wife, had one of the best rooms in our boarding house. Another couple, friends of theirs from Germany, had moved in at the same time. Their little boy, Billy, was the counterpart to Pipifax. The very name 'Pipifax' is a symbol of the child – eccentric, unusual, unnatural and always wanting everything different from other people.

When Billy's mother came to the kitchen and ordered noodles for her little boy, Pipifax's mother would say that her daughter wanted noodles too, but under no circumstances could she eat the same sort as Billy. Hers had to be cut much thinner, otherwise she would not touch them. When the other children had rice, she wanted cornflour. And when Billy ate his fresh fruit, she insisted on having hers stewed. In any case the stupid parents gave the child such quantities of sweets and chocolate between meals, that she could not possibly be expected to eat like a normal person at the proper times. But the mother, far from understanding that, kept on complaining that her child got such poor food that she would certainly fall ill.

I am quite sure that in their former life Pipifax's parents were reasonable and probably very charming people. But now robbed of their positions – they had both been doctors at a large hospital – they had lost their balance and were just nursing their grief, always expecting an insult and ready to defend themselves and, above all, their adored child. To make up for their daughter's loss of comfort they occupied themselves entirely with her. In fact by spoiling and coddling her they were doing a great deal of damage. They had made her the centre of everything: treating her appetite, her well-being and disposition as the most important thing on earth, and in doing so had made her self-centred and precocious. It seemed to me that the mother especially was looking for compensation for all the insults and injuries she had had to bear in Germany. She could not forget her position at the clinic, and she simply did not understand that here she was of just as much, or rather just as little, importance as everybody else.

At that time we did not imagine that the day would come when we were to long for Hänschen and Fritzchen, and to think fondly of Billy and Pipifax. We realized that even the naughtiest and most pampered child is pure pleasure compared to the really wicked spiteful characters who were soon to arrive.

The father, a well-known lawyer, had always been far too busy to look after the education of his sons, and did not really understand his wife or his children, as he knew them too little. I must confess, that for the first time in my life my experience in the treatment of people, and even of difficult people, proved entirely insufficient. When I first met the mother, a very good-looking woman, well-dressed and well-groomed, I was deeply impressed by her charm and good manners. But very soon I realized the mistake I had made. In spite of the lovely furs and clothes they had no money at all and were kept completely by the Committee, who paid us the lowest possible prices. But that did not prevent this family from demanding all sorts of extras and insisting on having the very best and the largest rooms in the house. The two boys were growing, and naturally had to have more and better food than all the others. They insisted on a breakfast of two eggs and much bacon. Of course they could eat nothing but brown bread, white bread not being substantial enough for them. They demanded jam, not marmalade, which they did not like at all. And only coffee, good strong coffee, such as they were used to in Vienna. They could not possibly drink tea. In the same way they had special wishes for lunch and dinner and were never content. But that was not the worst of it. The boys themselves surpassed everything else we had to put up with, they were real little gangsters, bent on ruining everything they saw. Both of them were technically minded, and nothing was safe when they were around. Be it a watch, they had to take it to pieces, or our typewriter, which we could never use again after they had finished with it. They ruined our bicycles and the sewing machine, losing all the important parts and not bothering to replace them. They spoiled our beautiful old furniture, using it for all sorts of gymnastic purposes, and worst of all, they tormented our animals. So it is not surprising that we considered it as good riddance when at last, after some months, the family went off to Australia. They had known from the very beginning that they would not be staying in this country, so they made not the slightest attempt to fall in with the customs of the land and to lead a decent quiet life.

Indeed, this is one of the chief difficulties which arose in connection with the refugee problem. There were always some who considered themselves only as through-travellers, with no obligations towards their temporary home. They did not respect the written and unwritten laws, but did as they pleased, and even boasted of it. They spoke loudly in their own language and behaved conspicuously in every way, never considering the harm they were doing to their fellow refugees who stayed in this country long after they had left and who would have to live down and make up for the bad impression the wanderers had created.

Of course it is never right to generalize too much. Sometimes we found our temporary visitors the best and most valuable persons, and we missed them greatly when at last they had to leave us. I am thinking especially of one family, whom we met shortly after the opening of our boarding house, and whom we grew to love almost passionately.

The man, a Viennese Jew, had married the daughter of a high officer, an aristocrat, and they had a charming boy of thirteen, who looked and behaved like a little prince. He loved my younger daughter with all his childish heart, and faithfully promised her that he would save all his pocket money and not spend a penny until he had enough to buy her a ticket to Sydney. We had some beautiful weeks with our friends, as if we had known each other all our lives. The moment we met we accepted each other, feeling and realizing our affinity. I had not been long in England and still had a good deal of natural, exuberant feelings and warm readiness for friendship. (Since then, the English climate and mentality which demand a certain reserve and cool balance, changed and to some extent subdued me. The longer one lives in a country the more readily and naturally one grows like its inhabitants.)

At that time we were very happy and lived a full rich life. We saw our friends every day after dinner. When we had all done our day's work they came to our kitchen and shared our simple meal: these fine distinguished people who would never lose their place, wherever they were.

Only after these dear friends had left us did the real everyday life in England begin. It was as if the last little piece of home had gone with them. After that we seemed to do nothing but say goodbye. People came and went – to America, to Bolivia, to Australia, everywhere.

At the beginning of the war this coming and going seemed to intensify. Those who were waiting to go to America and had counted on spending many months in England were called quickly and left us to try their luck in the new world. Even the situation of those who were staying in England completely changed. Once the Committee's funds were exhausted, most of the work was taken over by the British government. Some refugees had received permission to work; while others, especially the Czechs and Poles, joined the army and the pioneer corps in great numbers.

The worst grumblers were some of our old bachelors. They were miserable, feeling entirely useless, and therefore craved attention and flattery. If you took them seriously and considered their wishes they did not feel quite so futile and lost. They had nobody and nothing to think or to worry about – no wife, no occupation, no permit to work, not even hope for the future. So they wanted at least two things: respect and consideration. They felt and were unhappy, but they sought the reason for their

83

misery in external factors, such as their surroundings, their rooms and their food. They wanted changes, be it another form of diet, a new reading lamp, an additional blanket. They thought that they ought to have felt happy at last. Mrs Wilson and I both understood the reason for those rather useless and pathetic demands and patiently tried to fulfil them. We used to treat them like patients who already feel better at the first sight of the medicine bottle, even if it contains nothing but sugar water. Calmly we accepted their notice, which they gave us regularly – at least once a month – and listened to their explanations: that they really must have more quiet; that they required a stricter diet; or that they had decided to go into a nursing home. What they all needed – what would have cured all their many ailments – was a permit to work; then they would not have felt bored and useless. They would once again have a place and a purpose in life.

A permit to work can perform miracles, but also it can come too late, as in the case of our doctor, one of our oldest and best-loved guests. In Germany he was an eminent psychologist, and on his arrival in England he fully intended to continue his work, assuming he'd received permission to do so. And he was one of those lucky few who eventually was admitted to practise in this country. But a year or more had passed, and in the meantime our doctor had got used to a life of idleness, so that now he did not quite know what to do with his much-coveted permit. His lethargy, still aggravated by his high blood pressure, had damaged his capacity for work, although he had the best intentions of starting. But somehow he was not able to take the initiative. The first condition for a successful psychologist is the complete mastery of the language, and our doctor, who as a boy enjoyed a classical education, realized that he would be severely handicapped in this respect. Although he could read the papers and could generally express himself, his language skills were limited. In addition to this, he was middle-aged; his will and power to work were broken; he had not enough energy to start all over again, to learn a language and to build up a career at an age when normally he would be thinking of retiring. And even if he did succeed, would a few patients mean much security? And this security, what of it? Why and for whom should he try to gain it? Why all this struggle? He was a man of over fifty, without a family, without friends, quite alone in a strange country. Sometimes he wanted to do something, to feel useful again. But even this desire was not very strong: 'I am almost gone', he used to say, 'I don't really live any more in this world.'

He was quite happy if he solemnly and ceremoniously prepared his breakfast: by warming the coffee pot, taking a measured portion of coffee, a tiny pinch of salt, and filtering his favourite drink slowly and carefully. He usually finished this meal just when the gong for luncheon was sounded, and was always astonished and disappointed to find that his appetite had gone. So he found fault with our cooking, and wanted to correct its lack of flavour. A bit more sugar, some vinegar and red pepper, a little salt or caraway seed would have helped a lot to make the dishes more appetizing. (Our good Viennese cook already did rather too much in the way of spicing.)

But really, our doctor was an extremely kind and generous man, always ready to help. We had two old ladies, both over eighty, with us: my mother, whom I was very glad to get over from Germany, who shared a room with a childhood friend of hers. These two dear old ladies were always ailing. One would suffer from shortness of breath; the other from a bilious attack. Then the doctor was in his element. He would spend hours at their bedside, carrying hot-water bottles, fetching poultices and generally consoling them. Then the doctor of souls, who had for so long been dormant in him, came out again.

Altogether psychology is very necessary in a community of refugees. Each person has to try to help and understand the other. Always one or the other threatens to break down.

There was a middle-aged lady, an ordinary woman, whose husband was a professor at a university in southern Germany. These two had long been for all practical purposes separated. At home they occupied different apartments in their large house and sometimes did not see each other for weeks on end. Here they were forced to share one single room, and that with their 16-year-old son. In spite of being physically close to her husband, the poor woman was desperately alone. He had his own acute worries and troubles, and did not even notice her. He

85

did not know that she cried all night when she lay next to him, upset about the fate of her old father, having received no news of him since the outbreak of war. She found some consolation in her son, who worked as a trainee in a shoe factory. When he came home in the evening, tired and dirty, his first thought was always for his mother whom he worshipped. He always brought something for her – a flower, a cake or some sweets – anything he could afford. He felt that he must be everything to his mother: husband, father and son. At weekends he took her to the pictures, paying for this pleasure out of his own few pennies, leading her across the street, proud and happy.

Thus life went on for those three people, always very much in the same way. They tried to make the best of it, and hardly wanted other things. Then suddenly a new element stirred them up when a young married couple came to our boarding house. The man was Jewish, his pretty wife Aryan. But by a strange trick of nature the black-haired woman looked like a Jewess; while the man, with his blue eyes and fair hair, would have been taken for a pure Nordic type.

These two caused a real revolution. The man, Mr Miller, fell ill as soon as he arrived, and had to go to hospital with severe pleurisy. The young woman, feeling very lonely in these new surroundings, got to know the professor's wife very well and soon discovered that they both came from the same town. Common memories soon made the two women close friends, and when the professor's wife fell ill with a bad cold, and had to stay in bed, her new friend looked after her in a most unselfish manner.

The professor was sometimes present when she nursed his wife, but as usual he did not bother much with his surroundings. One day, by chance, he had a good look at young Mrs Miller and realized what a lovely, charming woman she was. He fell for her at once, and she quickly transferred her affection for the wife to the husband. Daily she accompanied him on his journey to the library and shared his futile hunt for a job. She went with him to his evening classes and took long walks with him on Hampstead Heath, in the light of the setting sun. They spent wonderful hours in the soothing beauty of Golders Hill Park, with its extravagant masses of daffodils and its old trees covered with the first dainty green of spring.

The return of Mr Miller burst like a bombshell in the midst of this idyll. He left the hospital much earlier than the doctors advised, driven by a mysterious inner discomfort and the certain feeling that there was something wrong with his wife. He could stand it no longer. Suddenly he appeared in the dining room. Silence greeted him as he entered. He looked around and saw the professor and his wife sitting at a small round table. He understood the situation immediately: it was not the first time that the pretty Mrs Miller had preferred a little excursion into *terra incognita* to the daily routine of her married life. His jealousy was increased by his fever and excitement and like a charging bull he ran towards these two. 'I won't touch a morsel in this house', he shouted. 'You have all conspired against me. You have let the professor seduce my wife, who is everything to me. I'd rather die of hunger and cold and illness than stay here a moment longer.'

And he meant what he said. Without her, life for him had lost its purpose. If he lost her he lost his very essence of life. What would happen to him, for surely she was going to leave him? She was set on regaining her freedom. His terrible jealousy and exaggerated possessiveness drove her away, so that she preferred a job as a cook to sharing her life with this man, who loved her so truly and passionately. For her, life with him was insupportable; for him, life without her had no meaning.

I could not help thinking of all these lonely women, who long for tenderness, for affection. What would they have given to belong to a man who loved them so sincerely. But nearly always love comes to the wrong house and knocks at locked doors that will not be opened.

Often we found many touching traits of generosity and sacrifice among the refugees. Many of them who could not really afford to, had acted as guarantors for their relatives, to save them from the unbearable hellish existence in Nazi Germany. They overworked in order to fulfil financial obligations towards relatives.

Such a person was a young lady who had been living with us for some time in order to recover a little after her hard work in a domestic setting. She had worked day and night to get her husband over here from Hamburg. She had acted as guarantor for him and had deposited all the money she had saved, including the amount she had received from selling her jewellery. Besides this, she had promised to pay one pound per week for him out of the 22 shillings she earned.

Just before war broke out she finally succeeded in getting him over. For weeks she had talked of nothing but him. When eventually I did see him, I was shocked. Not only was he weak and ugly – that would not have mattered much – but everybody, man or woman, who met him, had the same horrible impression of him and was disgusted and repelled. To me he seemed like a classic wideboy or black-market profiteer, who waits all day long for some shady business. The man was not honest. We all kept out of his way as much as we possibly could, and naturally had to give up all connection with his wife too, however much we liked her.

She pretended not to notice our changed attitude, not to feel the sudden emptiness around her. They both used to come and visit all her former friends, and behave as if everybody was delighted to see them. Even her oldest and truest friends who had known her all her life stayed away from her. And to think what she had done to bring him to England! She herself did not seem to be disappointed; or if she was, she did not show it. She called the ugly old man 'my darling dolly', and caressed him frequently and openly, while handsome, charming Mr Miller went begging to his wife for some little kindness, which she could not bring herself to give him. How capricious is love and full of whims!

One of our young women died, quite alone, far from all who were dear to her; indeed it was possible that her family in Germany did not even get the news of their only daughter's death. She was nineteen when she came to England, naturally as a domestic servant. With the outbreak of war she too had lost her job and had come to live at the hostel. She was quite happy with all the other young women, but somehow she always kept herself to herself. It was not in her to make friends easily. Since she had come to England she had always been poorly, and now her health gave way rapidly and she had to go to hospital. She was like a light that was slowly going out. She lacked the desire to go on living; she had given up all hope of ever seeing her parents again. She had lost her courage and really did not understand why she should put up a fight.

For several weeks this young woman lay there slowly dying. Her friends knew that she would never leave the hospital, and it was touching to see how they came every day and brought her flowers and fruit and did everything they could for her. None of these women had more than 1s 6d a week, and to buy flowers for their dying friend meant to go without even the smallest luxury – to renounce the weekly visit to the cinema, to do without cigarettes, sweets, even stamps. One of them came day after day, throughout the nine long weeks, and lavished love and attention upon the sick girl. She would not have missed a single visit, and did not feel happy unless she had seen her and tried to console her just a little.

The refugees were by no means all grumbling egoists. Those who stayed in England and settled down showed an astonishing amount of generosity and friendliness towards the others. Those who succeeded in getting their own flat, however small and primitive, were out of necessity hospitable and kept an open house. They welcomed friends and neighbours at all hours: those who lived in small and cold bedsits, with insufficient heating or none at all, hoping to warm themselves; and others who wanted to listen to the wireless or to have a plateful of hot soup or some coffee. The happy hosts, who were often finding it hard enough to manage anyway, and who probably did not know where next week's rent would come from, shared whatever they had with their visitors, even if it meant going hungry the next day.

It was pathetic to watch these people who wanted to settle in England and to see how hard they tried to adapt themselves to their surroundings, to learn the foreign language and to be as inconspicuous as possible. In the language classes which Bloomsbury House arranged for them you could meet distinguished old gentlemen and white-haired ladies of more than seventy trying to remember their words and competing for the place of star pupil. If one of them got too much attention they threatened a mutiny; a good mark made them happy and proud and meant more to them than it did in their schooldays. They had a great respect for their young teachers and at Christmas as a point of honour, they bought them little presents with their few pence.

It was naturally very important for the refugees to learn the language well, as only then could they hope one day to feel truly happy and at home here. So we would do our best to help them with their studies, suggesting that they went to lectures and to English churches. At the same time they got to know each other better, and that was all part of our intention: to create a real home for the refugees, where we looked after their souls as well as their bodies; where they could regain their peace and mental balance, and find people with similar interests and views. I am proud to say that many friendships which were started in and through our house lasted for life.

The idea of a real home had also been the chief point in our next enterprise: the domestic hostel. At the suggestion of Bloomsbury House, two of our homes were transformed into hostels for unemployed domestic servants, who before had lived in various places on their own. These girls and women, who were mostly quite alone in the world, wanted more than all the others to feel that they belonged somewhere. I truly believe that we succeeded in giving these homeless and often deeply unhappy people some feeling of security. They were able to make friends in the hostel where they found a circle of sympathetic people who made their loneliness less depressing and acute.

Nearly 50 domestic servants lived in the hostel: girls and women, aged between seventeen and fifty, from all social backgrounds. Most of them lost their jobs because of the war. In some cases the employers could no longer afford to keep servants; others closed their homes and after the departure of their sons or husbands went to live with relatives. A great many of them did not want to have a foreign woman, particularly a German, in the house.

The younger women had only one concern – to get away from the hated domestic service. They accepted every chance that could help them to do this, and so we saw a lot of them getting married rather hurriedly. Few of them were lucky enough to find an English husband who could solve all their problems. Generally the refugees intermarried among them-selves, and naturally these couples never had any money.

The most remarkable wedding was that of an unusually beautiful girl from our hostel with the manager of one of the departments of the domestic bureau. Dr Haber had an affidavit for America and was about to leave, when, a few weeks before his departure, he suddenly got scared of the loneliness and decided to take a wife across the sea, a companion for the uncertain future. He looked around in the hostel, the inhabitants of which he knew quite well through his work. From the very beginning Sonja had made a great impression on him, and so he asked her to come to his office, where without many explanations he asked her to be his wife and to go with him to America. 'Of course she will', thought Dr Haber. 'How could she prefer this miserable existence as a domestic servant to the pleasant and easy life as the wife of a capable man, who would immediately after his arrival in America find a good job and have a secure income.' He knew from experience that these uprooted and lonely refugee girls, even those from the best families, would take such an important step without much hesitation, and that they hardly ever considered this decisive change of their lives as carefully as they would have done under normal circumstances. So he was quite sure of Sonja as he waited for her to come to his office.

How great was his surprise – and his disappointment – when Sonja asked him for two days to make up her mind about his offer. He had not thought what her life had been like in the past, nor that her beauty might lead her to expect better offers in the future.

Sonja came to me, deeply upset, wanting my advice. Her life-story, which she told me, was interesting enough. She had a boyfriend in Italy, who sent her every day an ardent love letter and implored her to come to him, or in any case to wait for him. He was a handsome, fine youth, this Alfonso, rich and from one of the best families. He loved her with all his heart, but whether he would eventually be allowed to marry her was more than doubtful. His parents bitterly resented the idea and had already chosen a bride for him: an Italian girl of noble birth, who, having finished her education in a convent, had just come home. Sonja knew that they would never be able to break the resistance of his parents. But she was bent on marriage, if not to him then to somebody else. For this and no other reason she was considering

91

Dr Haber's offer. The phlegmatic, and in spite of his youth, rather stout man could not possibly bear comparison with her devoted young lover in Italy who had always been so generous and full of charm.

And there was something else: Sonja was not as lonely and unfortunate as many other refugee girls. She had a protector in England, a real lord. She had been to his house under unusual circumstances. Many years ago she had made his acquaintance when they were both present at an international sports conference in London. He had shown much kind interest in her and had given her his address, 'just in case'. She had remembered him in Vienna when she was desperately trying to think of a way out. She wrote to him, and immediately got the reply that he would obtain a permit for her as a domestic servant in his house, with a very good salary. So Sonja had come to London and was treated very well indeed. There were many staff in the house, and each one had to do just their own very specialized work. Sonja did little else except clean the silver. She had plenty of time for herself, in which she could go to the cinema, see her friends and learn English. At mealtimes the staff sat down to a well-laid table, and they were served by those on duty, like ladies and gentlemen. It was a small paradise.

But the outbreak of war put paid to Sonja's easy life. Her benefactor had to join his regiment; the house was closed and most of the servants, including Sonja, were dismissed. Now at last she too experienced the hardships of immigration and learned what it meant to be a servant, a refugee in a foreign country. She worked in different houses, where she had very much work and was poorly paid. She tried everything to find a suitable job, answered advertisements, advertised herself, but in vain. At last she came to the hostel, as after the outbreak of war it was almost impossible for a German girl to find a situation. It was here that Dr Haber first saw her, afterwards they had met once or twice in his office, and now, although he hardly knew her, he had asked her to marry him.

Sonja was in a very difficult position. What was she to do? Should she once and for all renounce hopes and dreams of Italian princes and English lords? Should she accept the proposal of an unromantic man who was going to take her far away to another part of the world?

After careful consideration I thought that I could, and should, advise Sonja to accept Dr Haber, as we all knew him as the most honourable and industrious man. So after the two days Sonja agreed to marry a comparative stranger and to follow him into another part of the globe, to start a new life. Such is the fate of the refugees.

We prepared a most splendid wedding for our lovely Sonja. The entire hostel took part. We considered this wedding as our own work and wanted to do something special for the occasion. The room was filled with flowers, a nice meal had been prepared and all the young women did their best to make things go well. They had produced a short play, *The Domestic Bureau as it is and as it Should Be*, which was a great success. They danced until the early morning and enjoyed themselves immensely. It was symbolic for them that one of their number, a domestic as they were, had found such happiness, such apparent luck. To them it seemed truly incredible to see their former colleague appear in a silver fox cape – the present of the proud bride-groom – and it gave them all new hope and trust in the future. Didn't they all expect to find the same good fortune one day?

Quite different was another wedding which took place shortly afterwards. This time a political refugee from Prague, who had stayed with us for a long time, married the woman to whom he had been engaged for many years and who had been his good and faithful comrade during the long and hard struggle. At last they had succeeded in escaping and had found protection and safety in hospitable England.

They were both quiet and serious people who had suffered much before they had reached their goal, and they did not really feel like celebrating. Nobody, not even their closest friends, knew about the wedding. I myself heard about it an hour before it took place, through my son-in-law, who was to be one of the witnesses.

At that time we had a small Ford car, and I asked my son-in-law to drive the couple to the Registry Office and to bring them back after the ceremony. Before they left I just had time to give the bride a large bunch of white lilies, and then these modest people, much to their own surprise, drove splendidly to their ceremony. It seemed to them the utmost luxury. They were so happy and grateful it made me feel almost ashamed. When they returned we had prepared a wedding breakfast, with some good things to eat and a few bottles of Australian wine, which we happened to have in the house. We played some records, danced to Viennese waltzes and this improvised celebration made us all very happy.

At this time we seemed to experience a romantic period, and one wedding followed another. Such joyous events naturally helped to make the lives of our young women happier and more cheerful.

Only those who have an aim can overcome obstacles, as they know what they are working for. They know that it is worthwhile, and that in the end they will be rewarded for all their troubles. They don't feel hunger and thirst and fatigue – no work is too hard for them. Several times we had groups of young *chaluzim* [pioneers] in our house. Young Zionist men and women who had worked on a farm and were now waiting for their certificates of emigration to Palestine. They used the time they had to spend in London to learn some practical skill, thinking of the country where they were going to build a free and happy life. They were not afraid of the hard work and little material gain that awaited them. They were building their future and the future of their children and grandchildren. They believed in that and this faith gave them the strength to bear all hardships lightly.

My daughter Puck was one of these young Zionists. As soon as she saw that our boarding house was established and could go on well without her help, she turned again to her favourite idea – her emigration to Palestine – and lived only for this goal. At first I was very sad at the thought of losing her. But when I read her first happy letters from Tel Aviv I knew that it would have been a great wrong to have tried to keep her back. Puck went her way and helped to build the Jewish renaissance.

The young Zionists were free from all the faults we saw in the other refugees. Their aim in life made them serious and quiet, even the youngest among them. This made them indifferent to hardship, uninterested in luxury and comfort. They wanted sufficient food, because they were mostly hard workers, physical workers, but they didn't care what you offered them and didn't think much about food. You could picture them clearly, building the roads and planting the orange trees in the land of their ancestors.

The political refugees from Czechoslovakia also had ideals, but unfortunately their goal was not as clear as that of the Zionists. Their lack of conviction sometimes made them prey to the usual refugee problems of indolence, divisiveness and lack of energy.

A great help and asset were the cultural clubs, which were founded for and by refugees: the Austrian Centre, the League of German Culture, the Lantern and others – cultural centres which provided a connection between artists and those who were interested in art. Here refugees could enjoy genuine German music and poetry, and were able to finally release themselves from bitterness and hatred of the Hitler regime in satirical political cabarets.

These communities played an important part in the life of the German and Austrian immigrants. They could spend many hours together, without being afraid of the waiter, who obviously found them a nuisance in the big cafés like Lyons. Here they could drink their beloved black coffee, could read all the papers they wanted, write letters, play chess and feel at home. But here they also had the chance to meet English people and to introduce the culture and art of their former countries.

Looking back on our refugee experience it seemed that a mutual exchange of national characteristics could only be beneficial. We, the Austrians, needed to find a way of understanding the feelings and souls of the English. We needed to try to find a way for an active interchange of thoughts and temperament. We had much to offer our English friends in terms of our easier ways and open friendliness, and from them we could learn exemplary discipline and self-control. The mixture should be a perfect one.

Tales from Berlin

IRENE KIRSTEIN WATTS

Irene Kirstein Watts responded to a letter that I had placed in the *Kindertransport Journal* requesting material for this book. She came to Britain on the *Kindertransport* [evacuation of children] of 10 December 1938. 'Tales from Berlin' is an autobiographical piece and was the first time she had fully explored writing about her early years in Berlin.

Irene is a writer/playwright for young audiences. She has lived in Canada since 1968.

In 1938 my parents Margot and Siegmund Kirstein managed to obtain a place for me on a *Kindertransport* going to England. I was seven years old. Such was the protectiveness surrounding me, that I never suspected that saying goodbye to parents, friends and family and travelling alone to a new country, was anything but a normal milestone in growing up.

In 1938 I was allowed to go to school alone. When I first began Grade 1 at the Jewish Kaliski School in Berlin my nurse-maid Cilly would take and fetch me. She always held my hand tightly, and hurried home, and wouldn't let us stop to look at anything – not even the window of the toyshop. It was a dream come true to go by myself. One day some big boys started shouting names at Cilly, and she seemed sad and cross. When we got home she was crying, and went to talk to Mutti in the dining room. They shut the door. Lotte, the housekeeper, gave me my snack at the kitchen table – bread and parsley butter, my favourite. Next day Mutti told me I was really too big to need Cilly any more, and anyway she was going home to get married. I said 'Who'll take me to school?' Mutti said, 'You may go alone!'

So I started to go to school by myself, but I didn't always go straight home. One day I went through the park, not just outside by the railings, and sat on the bench. It had writing on the

96

back of it. I traced the letters with my finger. They said '*Juden Verboten*', I could read that. I sat there and stared at the park-keeper and swung my legs (I had my horrible brown lace-up boots on) and ate every bit of my apple that I hadn't eaten at lunch-time. Then I went home. Nobody asked me what I had been doing. Another time I watched a parade. It was right by Unter den Linden where we lived. It was a lovely day, the sky was very blue and there were bright red, white and black flags waving; the soldiers' boots shone in the sun, and they lifted their legs high. The band was playing. I wanted to sing, and I crawled right through to the very front of the crowd and saw girls, not much bigger than me, with pleated skirts and white blouses, and they were marching too. The people put out their arms and saluted the man in brown standing in a big open car – I knew his face. I thought Hitler looked very nice (I didn't know why Vati said he was a *schweinhundt*), and all the people were so happy. The man standing beside me smiled at me and patted my head, then I went home. I never told anyone I'd saluted.

When I got home there was a big surprise. Vati had come home. He'd been gone for a long time. He was sitting in a green velvet chair in front of the window, he had his dressing-gown on, even though it was daytime - his hair was cut very, very short. I wanted to touch it, but I didn't. I think he was crying – I had never seen him cry before – and for a minute I wanted to go away, but Mutti said quickly, 'Look what Vati has brought you from his holiday – marzipan. You can eat it now.' Marzipan was my absolutely favourite food – even better than the boiled egg I had for Sunday breakfast. I said, 'Where did you go for your holiday, Vati?' He said, 'Konzentrationlager', or something like that. I went out to play. It was not until many years later that I discovered he had been imprisoned. (My mother had bought the sweets for him to give to me.)

Next day in school at news-time, Richard cried. He said, 'My father has been taken to the concentration camp.' A lot of the children shouted: 'And mine'. I felt proud. I said, 'That's nothing. My Father went and he came back and brought me a present!' I was glad I could comfort Richard. Herr Müller smiled at me, and I was happy.

That night Mutti said there was going to be a goodbye party for the whole class. We would have hot chocolate and cakes, and a puppet show. The school was closing, even though we hadn't finished the first class yet, and soon I would go on a long holiday, very far away. We had the party, and a photographer came and took a picture of us all. The mothers looked sad, only Herr Müller was making jokes. Soon after that Mutti told me about the holiday plans. I was going to England. I supposed we were all going together. Mutti showed me pictures in a magazine of two little girls. They were English princesses and I had a coat just like theirs! Then we went to visit a dressmaker, right over the other side of the city. I was going to have lots of new dresses for England. The dressmaker said I must have a dress right down to the ground, because in England there were garden parties and I would need a long dress. It was blue. After that the days went very fast and I couldn't count how many people I said goodbye to. At last it was time to pack, but instead of the new suitcases full of clothes, toys and books, Mutti said I was only allowed one case for the journey, so that I could manage to carry it myself. We put in the party dress, but I never wore it. Mutti made me wear three sets of underwear. Three vests and three knickers, and scratchy wool stockings. She said England was cold. I was sweating.

At the station, all the children looked bigger than me. I didn't know anyone, Mutti held my hand very tightly, and Vati carried my case. I held Freddy, my new Kathe Kruse doll with the blonde hair.

All the grown-ups looked as if they were crying. I didn't know why – wasn't this a holiday? I asked, 'Where's Lotte? She'll be late.' Mutti said in a funny voice, 'She had to go to the dentist, she'll see you soon.' And then I knew she wasn't coming. Nobody at all was coming with me. Then it was time to go. Vati helped me into the train and shut the door. I don't remember kissing my parents goodbye. I knelt on the seat and leaned out of the window, and Freddy and I waved. Vati waved a white handkerchief, and the train went faster and faster. I was going to England. A strange lady next to me told me her name, and said we could keep each other company, and that we would be going on a boat! I lifted up my skirt and took off my scratchy stockings. I couldn't wait to go to England to take off my three sets of underwear.

The Spies

IRENE KIRSTEIN WATTS

'The Spies' is a humorous story about Irene Kirstein Watt's evac-
uation to Wales – 'There was a moment when I did believe the
men talking about Hitler were spies, but even at the age of nine
I knew I was stretching the truth in order to get attention. It felt
wonderful to be in the spotlight.'

Mr and Mrs Williams, my foster parents, had requested a
blonde, four-year-old girl. They got me, a nine-year-old with
light brown, straight hair and an unpronounceable name. They
gave me a bedroom of my own, removing the rubber sheets on
the bed a little sadly. Lace mats covered every item of furniture
except for the bed, which had a pink silk eiderdown. There was
nothing to do. I read Auntie's copies of *Woman's Own*, and puz-
zled over the answers in the advice columns. My cousin, who
looked like Shirley Temple, had a much more interesting billet.
Each night, after supper, she was made to tickle her foster
father's feet. The story leaked out, and she was soon returned to
London.

'Uncle Gwilym is an important man', said Auntie Lilian. 'He
is Assistant Manager at the National Provincial Bank. He has his
own office.' I could not imagine Uncle Gwilym with bare feet –
he was always dressed in a grey suit.

Uncle Gwilym and Auntie Lilian had no children. They introduced me to exotic foods like jelly and lava bread, which looked
like seaweed but tasted delicious. They taught me the words of
the Welsh national anthem and showed me off lovingly to their
friends. 'This is Irene, our little evacuee.' The ladies whispered
amongst themselves before turning to me: 'There that's nice,
and how do you like being Auntie Lilian's little girl?' I would
blush and nod shyly. What did they expect me to say? Then I
sang in Welsh, watching Auntie's proud smile.

On my way home from school, I always walked as slowly as possible. One afternoon I eavesdropped on two men talking intently. They looked foreign to me. They wore heavy boots, white mufflers and cloth caps. They spoke very fast in a 'foreign' language. I made out the word 'Hitler'.

Spies plotting!

I hurried to Uncle's bank. He came from behind the counter right away. 'Hello, *bach* – shouldn't you be going home for your tea?' 'Uncle, I heard some spies talking.' 'Spies indeed! What are you saying? Come with me quick, away from the customers.' He led me to a box-like room – his office. 'Now what is all this? Spies in Llanelli, are you sure?' I was becoming more sure every minute. 'Oh, yes. They said they were landing on the coast. I heard them say 'Hitler'. I didn't understand everything.' Uncle Gwilym took my hand. 'Can you show me where you saw them?' Off we went, driving down the high street. 'Over there', I said, 'by the phone box. They're gone now.' Uncle asked me if I'd recognize them again. I assured him earnestly that I would. We drove around the town and, at intervals, I'd point to some innocent, booted miner and say, 'That looks like them.' Uncle Gwilym never doubted me for a moment. 'We'll go to the police station and report', he said. I was supremely confident. I knew I had uncovered a great crime. Didn't all the posters and billboards warn us that 'Walls have ears'? Well, I'd certainly overheard something.

Sergeant Jones, large, red-faced and very kind, said, 'Now then, *bach*, don't be frightened, I'm just going to take down the particulars.' I wasn't in the least bit frightened – in fact I was having a very good time indeed. When would I be fingerprinted?, I wondered.

By the time Sergeant Jones had finished asking me questions, and had carefully written down the answers, the spies had acquired ominously distinctive features, and their conversation included references to raids, parachutes and secret meeting places. No one thought to ask me what language the spies spoke. It was assumed that they were speaking German – a language that I had carefully suppressed in a year and a half of trying to turn myself into a proper English girl. Did no one even consider that the 'foreign language' might have been Welsh?

'*Dioch yn fawr*, Irene. Thank you very much. Be sure to let your uncle know if you see the men again.'

It was over. That weekend Uncle began to work on a shelter in the garden. I helped him paint the inside walls pink. From time to time, I would say, 'I think I saw those men again.' It hadn't begun as a lie, rather an idea that grew, as stories do. I had not yet learned to separate fiction from the truth.

Land of My Father

IRENE KIRSTEIN WATTS

Irene Kirstein Watts' parents arrived in England in the spring of 1939, her father having recently been released from Sachsenhausen concentration camp. He was almost immediately interned as an enemy alien. Poorly advised, he had informed the tribunal that he hoped to return to Germany after the war. He was sent to the Isle of Man and was subsequently transported to Australia on the infamous ship *Dunera* and returned to Britain in 1943. Living in Llanelli he worked on a market-stall, owned by one of the well-to-do Jewish 'matrons', selling bolts of cloth. 'Land of My Father' is about him.

My father was a salesman. Shoulders bowed, a beak of a nose, thinning hair.

He always wore mourning clothes: grey suit, sleeve turned to hide the fraying cuffs. Black tie, pearl pin (real). White shirt with detachable stiff high collar. Black shoes, polished each night to brilliance, over socks he darned himself.

His speech, thickly accented, made chaos of syntax. German and Yiddish crept in.

Men and women, friends and strangers were addressed indiscriminately as 'darlink'.

I blushed for him, wished he were a miner – someone else.

Father left home punctually each morning at six, to catch the tram to the railway station.

Home now was 5 Murray Street, Llanelli, South Wales. Three rooms and an attic rented from the Prudential Insurance Company below us.

The Prudential closed at 5 p.m. After the cleaner left I wandered through the offices. Once in an unlocked desk I found a photograph of a bare-bosomed woman. It was an interesting place.

The secretary left, and her affair with the manager, a married man, was hushed up. The cleaner found him dead, hanging in the broom closet. The doors were kept locked after that.

My father's customers were spread through towns with exotic names: Mumbles, Swansea, Carmarthen, Merthyr.

He travelled by train. Unlike Willy Loman he had no car and did not know how to drive. He carried his jewellery line in a heavy sample-case, and worked on commission only. 'I don't want to sell you anything, only take a look.' He fooled nobody, but got in everywhere just the same, he told us, adding up orders in his notebook.

Returning long after dark, he changed into a once-elegant brown quilted robe and ate leftover supper, lavishing praise for the fried potatoes my mother cooked for him. He patted her arm lovingly with his delicate white hands, smooth from their Sunday manicure. Each Sunday, after lunch he soaked and filed and clipped. The sound more irritating even than the snoring nap that followed.

His neatness was a fetish. Every piece of string, each brown sheet of wrapping paper, was folded and put away.

Before his death, he made the beds, tidied the rooms. He sent my mother on an outing, and covered the gap under the kitchen door with blankets. He had selected his own gas oven, adding a new label to those he bore already: Jew, Concentration Camp Victim, Refugee, Enemy Alien, Internee, Commercial Traveller, Survivor, Suicide.

The orthodox Rabbi buried him grudgingly in ground set apart from more righteous Jews who had lived out their normal spans.

My mother and I were the only mourners.

The same Rabbi called soon after, to offer Mother comfort (physical and financial) and a silent partnership. (We wondered if his wife was silent too.) His plan was to open a kosher butcher shop – a sound investment – using my father's savings.

After he left, Mother wiped away tears of mirth and hysteria.

She grieved amongst decaying bouquets and cards from strangers, customers who wrote respectfully, 'With love'.

The Portrait

LOTTE MUNZ

My grandmother, Lotte Munz, came to Birmingham in 1937 from Karlsruhe. For many years she taught German at a nearby private girls' school, but once she retired she began writing. 'The Portrait' is one of the short stories that she wrote in which she describes the apartment that she had lived in with my grandfather, mother and aunt. A few years after her death in 1984 I placed copies of her stories in the Wiener Library in London. Then in November 2000 my mother received a telephone call from an artist, Polly Rockberger, who had come across the story, 'The Portrait', and on reading it had been inspired to paint a semi-abstract picture of the room described in the story. The painting is now in my possession.

The living room of the spacious flat in the centre of a south German town had originally been designed as a ballroom for a wealthy businessman, but the young Jewish ear, nose and throat surgeon who moved in with his family had decided to turn it into a comfortable and elegant place.

It was a November afternoon in 1938.

The windows which faced the balcony were closed, the curtains half drawn, but the furniture and shape of the room could be distinguished.

Two brown marble columns reached up to the ceiling and two marble balustrades divided a rounded recess from the main part of the room. This served as a conservatory. A heron with spread wings was suspended from the ceiling and moved slowly over a round table and two wicker chairs. The mosaic stone floor was covered with a Persian rug. The houseplants, in window-boxes in the bay, looked well cared for. The brass birdcage was empty. The door was open. There was some water left in the little bowl.

The Portrait

The impression of grandeur was lessened by a very thought-ful arrangement of the furniture. A black piano was placed towards the centre of the room. The wide, inlaid oak floor was almost covered with the red Persian carpet. A cleverly designed built-in settee formed a corner and made the room appear even smaller. It was framed by oil paintings and engravings. A table with a tablelight was set for two. On the opposite wall stood a low, carved bookcase, with a traditional menorah on top. A stan-dard light and three comfortable easychairs invited one to sit down and read. A few crumpled cushions were scattered around and increased the impression of a hasty departure. The walnut writing desk, near the window, was decorated with fam-ily photographs. A letter with an English stamp, the address written in a boyish handwriting, was still unopened. The two double doors on either side of the room, were closed. A brass chandelier, suspended from the ceiling, helped also to minimize the size of the room. The Old Testament, beautifully bound in red and gold, was placed on a sewing table.

What gave this place its distinction was the life-size portrait of a gentleman. He sat in a high-backed chair, wearing a con-ventional dark suit, his legs slightly crossed, holding his hat with his left hand. His delicate features were framed by a well-groomed, light brown beard; his kind face expressed sympathy and knowledge of human suffering and a very slight strain of sadness. His light brown eyes looked straight into the room. The most expressive part of the painting were his small nimble hands, the fingertips a little turned upwards: a surgeon's hands.

The noise of the trams and cars from the main street did not penetrate up to this second-floor flat.

Suddenly there was a terrific crash. The door was pushed open. A group of men in brown uniform, jackboots and red swastika armbands stormed in. They tore the windows wide open, pulled down the curtains and then, the first one seized the beautiful white and blue vase, which stood on the piano and threw it out of the window. The second one had an axe: with it he smashed the piano to pieces. Another one took some chairs and threw them down into the street; yet another slit up the settee.

One of them hesitated for a second. The portrait with the knowing eyes seemed to look directly into his brutal face. The small scar behind his ear – the result of a complex surgical operation – reddened. His face became distorted. Then he took from his belt a big army knife, climbed onto a chair, and slashed the picture to pieces.

It was all the work of a few minutes. After they had destroyed it all, one of them said, 'Orders obeyed. Now let's go and have a glass of beer.'

Quo Vadis?

ANDREW HERSKOVITS

Andrew Herskovits was deported to Auschwitz and eventually
liberated in Belsen. In this country he has worked as a teacher
and is now a hotelier. He leads a creative writing group which
has met once a week for the last ten years at the Holocaust
Survivors' Centre, in Hendon, north London.

'I love April sunshine,' smiled Adele, 'hot weather doesn't agree
with me.'

'I'm going to Greece next August. The hotter the better for
me.' Celia was twenty-eight and she was going to take over one
of Adele's clients.

'At your age I was a sun-worshipper, too; now I can't take the
heat. But it's such a lovely day, isn't it?'

'The first sunny day this year,' agreed Celia.

'Is this where Mrs Bollman lives?'

The two social workers had stopped outside the old canalside
house. The older woman, Adele, nodded and rang the bell.

'Who is it?' asked the voice on the intercom.

'Hello Dorothea. It's Adele. Can we come up?'

The buzzer let them in and they climbed up the narrow stairs
to the first floor. The door of the flat was opened by a lady in her
sixties with a slim figure and a face whose fine bone-structure
had preserved it from the furrows of age. She wore a black silk
dress with a white belt and black and white court shoes. Her fingers were manicured, her hair well-groomed. To Celia, the
young social worker, Mrs Bollman didn't seem to need special
care.

Mrs Bollman smiled. 'Please sit down ladies.'

The room was softly lit by table lamps with pink and white
silk shades. After the introductions Celia asked: 'Can I call you
Dorothea too?'

'Of course. I am no trouble, am I Adele? I shan't be to you either Celia.'

'Of course not; we'll be friends. I like your dress! And what lovely hair you have, like spun silver!'

'I had auburn hair; I was thirty-two when it went white … '

'That was very young … '

'But there are no black tulips, it's only the light … '

Celia caught the frown on Adele's face and realized that she might have been unintentionally indiscreet. Wanting to ease the atmosphere she went over to the window: 'It's sunny outside; let me draw the curtains for you.' She did so, revealing thick boards nailed to the frames blocking the windows.

'Don't do that!' Dorothea cried, her face contorted with fear. 'We mustn't show even a chink of light!'

Celia closed the curtains again. 'I am sorry.'

'She's very young,' Adele hastened to explain, 'she doesn't realize the danger.'

'Yes,' Dorothea said, 'she's very young. Would you like some cocoa?'

'That would be lovely,' said Adele, and the two social workers watched as their client pottered in and out of her kitchen, finally presenting a jug of steaming cocoa on a cloth-covered tray. They chatted about the royal families of Holland, Belgium, Spain and England – a subject on which Dorothea was both knowledgeable and voluble. When they stood up to leave, Celia was intrigued by her new client.

'What was that about her hair?' she asked as they were making their way down the stairs.

'It's a long story,' said Adele.

'I suppose I can read it up in her file … '

'I think I am the only person who knows. I went to school with Peter, one of her sons.'

'I thought she had no relatives.' There was no reply from Adele. 'Has it something to do with the boarded-up windows?' Celia asked. 'Please … '

'It's a sad story, Celia … you needn't know.'

'I want to know.'

'It'll upset you.'

'It's upsetting you too. I want to know … '

'Let's go to the café across the road.'

Quo Vadis?

Stirring sugar into her espresso, Adele began: 'I was fifteen. The Germans had begun rounding up Resistance fighters and Jews, there were raids in railway-stations, hotels ... I knew the Bollmans were in hiding, Peter and I ... well, he was my best friend ... '

'You loved him?'

'Yes, I loved him.'

'Oh Mother, don't be a spoil-sport!'

'Don't you realize that as soon as you leave the cellar, you are in danger?'

'But Dorothea, my dear,' said the Poodle, 'we have pure Aryan papers ... '

'If they're so good, why must we hide? They may be better than nothing, but they are forgeries. It's not worth risking your lives to see a film!'

'But it's *Quo Vadis?* Mother,' insisted Peter.

'Please Mother, we've been here six weeks,' pleaded ten-year-old Tom.

'It's dark outside,' said the Poodle, 'I've grown a moustache and when they hear my *Hochdeutsch*, they'll take me for an SS *Obersturmbannführer* in disguise.'

Dorothea gazed at her husband with a mixture of love and exasperation. His once curly black hair was now flecked with grey, but the nickname 'Poodle', which she had given him on the day they had first met in Heidelberg, had stuck. Ever since then, his blue eyes had followed her more faithfully than a poodle. He was always punning and joking, and while normally she would have reacted to his facetiousness with forbearance, today she found it offensive.

'You're not going out to risk the boys' lives for some old film! No, no and no!' Mrs Bollman was only 5 ft 2 ins, with a slim, delicately rounded figure, thick auburn hair and huge black eyes that normally radiated sensuality and humour. But she had an iron will, and when those black eyes clouded over and flashed fire, as they did now, the Poodle hung up his hat.

'Practise your irregular English verbs,' she told Tom. 'Yesterday you wrote: 'I goed to school ... ' Then she sat down by the lamp on the little round table to continue her reading of *Anna Karenin*.

109

David Bollman who was forty-two, ten years her senior, watched his beloved wife's head haloed in the soft glow of the lamp. He ached for her, especially as they had had no privacy since they had moved into the cramped cupboard-sized cellar to escape deportation to Germany. After reading a while Dorothea closed her eyes. Poor little Alexei, how unhappy he must be, abandoned by his mother, his father cold and distant. A sense of stifled sobs penetrated her consciousness, as if the little Russian boy, Alexei, were weeping. She looked up, couldn't see Tom, but now recognized his weeping and traced it to the old blanket-chest at the foot of the bed where all four of them slept. He was curled up inside, crying.

It was in their first flat, ten years before when all this began. Tom had a sweet tooth and she had hidden a box of Belgian chocolates on the top shelf of a bookcase; she was in the kitchen when the loud crash startled her; rushing in to the lounge she had found Tom sitting among the books and broken china, munching bon-bons. Terrified of the damage he might have done to himself, she smacked his little leg and shouted at him; then, still upset, she righted the cabinet and began to clear up the mess.

Suddenly she smelt it! She rushed into the kitchen, to find the veal escalopes black and smoking, but it was while scrubbing the frying-pan that she missed Tom, who was usually in and out of the kitchen, chattering to his toys and asking her innumerable questions.

'Tom?' Silence. 'Tom?' Silence. 'Where are you, Tom?'

Concerned, she went into the lounge; then into the boys' bedroom, the bathroom. Then, her heart beating faster, she went into her own bedroom. She looked for him frantically every-where. She thought she heard a little sound from one of her wardrobes, so she flung it open – and there was the little monkey. She snatched him up in her arms and kissed his tears away. After that, whenever he thought he was in trouble, Tom always hid somewhere to punish himself in the dark.

Now, she looked at her son through tear-misted eyes. She smiled at him, got up and took the boy's cap and coat from the hanger.

'Go and see your film.' Turning to her husband, she added, 'Be careful, Poodle. Here's some money, buy the boys ice-cream.'

She checked that they all put on their scarves – it was December. At the trap-door she kissed them all.

'What time does the film end?'

The Poodle grinned. 'At midnight when, like Cinderella, we all disappear.'

'I'll collect you,' she said. (She hated his silly joke.)

'You don't have to, mother,' whispered Peter.

'The fresh air will do me good.'

When they had gone, she prepared the supper of bread, cheese and onions with which to welcome her family. Then she sat down again with *Anna Karenin*.

Three hours had flown by unnoticed, and in the book Anna was now alone and in total despair. There was no one in her life who loved her. Dorothea condemned the faithless wife, the mother who gave up her son for her lover, yet the tears welled up in her eyes for the lonely woman.

At 15 minutes to midnight she put the page-marker in the book, although there were not many pages left. She put on her scarf and coat, switched off the light and left the cellar by the hidden trap-door.

As she made her silent way up the dark stairwell, she felt suddenly terrified. Had someone touched her? An icy hand gripped her heart and squeezed until she could not breathe and had to sit down on the stairs and mop the cold sweat from her forehead. There was something frightful echoing in her mind, like a distant funeral bell. She listened, holding her breath, her heart banging away in her chest like a mad drummer.

She forced herself to be calm; there was no one there; she had to collect her family.

Outside in the street it was snowing. Amsterdam was determined, despite the war, to have a cheerful Christmas. There were fir trees in the windows, with candles and sweets wrapped in coloured paper. The lit-up rooms were only half-hidden by curtains. How cosy, how safe and happy were those people inside. How lucky not to be Jews!

It was a short walk to the cinema. The foyer was in semi-darkness. The film would end in about ten minutes and the cashier had already gone home, leaving the uniformed attendant pacing up and down like a caged animal.

Presently a couple emerged, he put up an umbrella against

111

the driving snow and they hurried away. Others followed and Dorothea came near so as not to miss them, looking at every face until there were no more faces. The attendant went to the glass doors to lock up when she approached him.

'There was a *razzia* [raid],' he replied to her enquiry, 'the Germans were looking for the Resistance, they checked everyone's papers. Was your husband with two young lads? They were arrested.'

The woman stepped outside to let the attendant lock up and stood there as if rooted in the pavement, rigid like a statue.

'I am sorry,' muttered the man as he turned and walked away. Half-way home he stopped and went back. The bells of the Church of Saint Teresa had begun to toll midnight when he turned the last corner and saw her still there.

'Are you all right?' he asked. 'Where do you live?'

She didn't seem to hear him.

The two women waited around the corner from the office block where they could see the cinema. It was early April and a cold wind was blowing. Adele looked at her watch.

'Ten to midnight.'

Celia shivered and wondered how she herself would cope with the death of her husband and children, if she lost them. (Bollman and the boys had died in Auschwitz.)

There were no passers-by in the street at this hour so they could hear the shuffle of feet before they saw the small solitary figure walking towards the cinema.

'Is that Dorothea?' asked Celia in a shocked whisper. She couldn't recognize the attractive, middle-aged lady she had met earlier in this old woman with bent shoulders. Adele could only nod. Why can't I ever get used to this sight? she demanded of herself. It's time I left this job, I'm too sentimental.

The old woman stopped outside the cinema.

The lights went on in the foyer and a young couple emerged into the street; the man turned up his collar, she took his arm and they hurried away home. As others came out, the woman scrutinized every passing face until the attendant brought her a cup of something steaming hot.

'Her cup of cocoa,' whispered Adele.

The attendant stayed talking until she finished it, then took the empty cup, shook hands with the woman and went back into the foyer. In a few seconds the lights went off. The attendant locked the doors, waved to her and went away.

The old woman looked up at the sky and, as if in answer, the bells of the church of Saint Teresa began to toll. Her shoulders sagged, her head hung lower as she walked slowly away from the cinema. At the twelfth stroke she turned the corner and was gone.

Memories

ROSE ELLIS

Rose Ellis was born in Germany. Her father died, following a Nazi attack; and when her mother fled to Belgium, Rose was left in Germany with friends as she was due to join a *Kindertransport* to England. At the age of thirteen she was left alone in Germany as her friends had emigrated. Her mother then arranged for her to move to Belgium. After the German invasion they came to England.

Rose Ellis was also a member of the creative writing group in Hendon.

'Sorry,' called the orderly through the open lounge door. 'Rita won't be able to come today.'

The disappointment was plainly visible on the faces of the half dozen people who had been eagerly awaiting their weekly quiz with Rita. Her questions gave them a chance to test their memories, to prove to others and to themselves that the dreaded Alzheimer's disease which was stalking their retirement home had not yet put its finger on them. Rita's quizzes were a challenge and a pleasant pastime. She took care not to overtax her Jewish dears, as she called them. No questions from the New Testament, none about modern technology and preferably none that would produce argumentative debate. Rita was very good at her job. She employed humour to smooth ruffled feathers – and feathers in the old people's home were easily ruffled.

In her absence this Wednesday, her devotees sat with hands idly in their laps, staring forlornly out of the windows on to a rain-sodden lawn framed by a grey and hostile sky.

Normally, Mrs Berman would painstakingly try to add a few stitches with her arthritic fingers onto a small embroidery frame she always carried around with her and which never seemed to

114

get finished.

'Oh, that rain,' she moaned. 'It's killing me. My arthritis is worse than ever.'

Mrs Kober, who could usually be seen carrying a book around her (preferably with a highbrow title in which the bookmark seemed to forever remain on the same page), enquired, 'Do you think they are related?'

'Of course they are related,' retorted Mrs Berman.

Mrs Heller, who could never resist the temptation of putting the cat amongst the pigeons, asked archly: 'On which side?'

Mrs Berman answered, sounding annoyed: 'It's not my side. It's all up my arm, right down to my fingertips.'

Mrs Roberts took the opportunity to prove that she was on the ball, by commenting: 'She doesn't mean the side of your body.'

'I don't know from which side of the family I got the arthritis. All I know, it's killing me.'

By now Mrs Heller was finding the conversation tedious. 'Why all this talk about pains and aches? Surely there are far more interesting subjects to discuss?'

'Such as?' enquired a still aggrieved Mrs Berman, whose main interests were pains and aches, but unlike those of the medical profession, her concerns were only for her own ills.

Mrs Heller looked down her long legs stretched out in front of her, still slender and shapely, not like those on either side of her that resembled tree trunks. Her legs were her reminder that she had once been young and desirable. Looking up she said impishly: 'What's wrong with talking about love, romance and passion?'

The others, initially startled by the reference to things deemed to be long in the past, were obviously giving the subject some thought. Mrs Berman momentarily straightened her shoulders and stretched her neck, whilst Mrs Roberts moved her head, as if trying to toss an invisible curl back into place. Once many curls had adorned her head. Now, sadly, they were replaced by thin, white strands that barely covered her skull.

The women all remained silent. Their eyes seemed to focus inwards as if they were opening secret doors in their heads.

Mr Feldmann, the only male amongst the clutch of hens, had remained quiet throughout this bizarre chatter. He always tried to stay aloof from the females in the home. He would never choose a seat right next to any of them and when asked why not, his standard reply was: 'I don't want to show favouritism.'

It was almost two years after his wife's death that he had entered the home. Though still fit and mobile, he found it hard to manage on his own, having been spoilt by a devoted wife who had looked after him like a mother. He had never been asked to help with any household chores, and he had never volunteered. To be looked after in the home suited him, provided the ladies left him alone. He would often sit with them in the lounge, needing to escape from the confines of his own room. Usually he kept his eyes closed, not because he was asleep, but in order to avoid being spoken to.

When he heard Mrs Heller throw out the challenge to speak of romance and passion, as if by magic, Rosa's face appeared behind his closed lids. Rosa, the girl he had last seen more than 50 years earlier.

It was 1942, when they were both staying in a run-down lodging house on the outskirts of Paris. It was a bad year during which Hitler's henchmen were relentlessly rounding up the remnants of Jews still to be found in France.

He had passed her a few times on the staircase and had realized instinctively, without speaking, that they shared a common heritage and were victims of the same hate. They had both registered under false names, hoping that they would never see the jackboots of the Gestapo or hear the shrill whistle of the French militia.

That night, so vivid still in Mr Feldmann's mind, they had both arrived at the same time at their respective rooms on the first floor when the sound of commotion downstairs had made the girl shake uncontrollably, so that she was unable to fit the key in the doorlock. He had gone over to help when she had turned to him, whispering: 'I am so afraid. I don't want to be alone. Please may I stay with you?'

Leading her to his room he had felt her body quiver under her thin clothing. During the night she had clung tightly to him, as if she thought it her last chance to experience passion and to know love. The touch of her body had stayed in his mind and now, even his tired limbs remembered. Yet all he ever knew about her was that her name was Rosa, that she was nineteen years old and what she had felt most was fear and what she craved desperately was to know love.

The next morning he had left early whilst she was still asleep in his bed. He had gone to try and sell a few more of his belongings so that henceforth there would be enough money to cover both their immediate needs for the time being. When he returned just a short while later, he found that what she had dreaded so much had actually come to pass. The militia had called and had taken her away, and all he knew was her first name. The name on the register had been false and though he had spared no effort to trace her long after the war, he had never found her again. Later he married, had children and had felt love for his wife who would also have a place in his heart, but when there was talk of passion and romance the picture his mind would produce would always be that of Rosa, so young, so vulnerable, her black hair spread on his pillow, as he had last seen her.

He opened his eyes and looked at his companions sitting stiffly in their armchairs wondering whether any of these ladies, now old, had ever been a Rosa in a young man's life.

Extracts from Coming Home

CHAIM BERMANT

Chaim Bermant, celebrated writer, novelist and journalist, was born in Poland in 1929. He came to Glasgow at the age of eight.

Coming Home was written after he and his family had returned to England having spent a significant period of time living in Israel. There had been difficulties that had made it hard for him to write, namely the Yom Kippur War, and also the fact that his wife, Judy, had been seriously ill. She had wanted to stay, but, as Judy Bermant said, 'writing for him was almost more important than anything else. He had to write.' And writing was difficult for him in Israel.

The book *Coming Home*, published in 1976 (now out of print), came out of that experience. It was an attempt to make sense out of all his early childhood experiences as well as his later life choices, in particular, living in Israel. The following chosen extracts focus on his childhood in Latvia and the family's move to Glasgow in 1937.

Chaim Bermant died in 1998.

Barovke

Latvia, Lithuania, Poland! They had until 1918 all been part of Russia, and Jews still moved from one to the other as if there was no frontier, sometimes with the necessary permits, not infrequently without. My parents were Russian. In 1918, as a result of the Brest–Litovsk Treaty which gave Poland and the Baltic states independence, they became Lithuanian. Two years later Poland seized the Lithuanian province of Wilno [Vilnius], and they became Polish. Jews were used to changes of identity as they moved back and forth across Europe, but at this time one could change merely by standing still.

I was born in 1929 in Breslev, a frontier town just inside Poland, and three years later my father was invited to become Rabbi of Barovke, a village over the border in Latvia.

My father, like my mother, was always reticent about his age and early history. He was bearded for as long as I had known him and always looked old, and I found it difficult to imagine him as a young man or a boy. His father, a short, stocky, genial man with smiling eyes and a large white head who looked like every child's idea of Santa Claus, and who was something of a Santa Claus by temperament, was a pedlar who even in his old age trudged on foot through the great forests with a pack on his back selling haberdashery to woodsmen and charcoal-burners. He could never make a living, but never seemed to be troubled by the fact, and whenever he visited Barovke the house seemed to glow with his presence. My father, who was the second of three sons, inherited much of his amiability but nothing of his carefree spirits, and during those rare periods of his life when he had no real worries he was – like my mother – consumed by pseudo-worries. He was by inclination, temperament and training a scholar, and had been sent as a young man to Slobodka, perhaps the foremost seat of Talmudic learning in Eastern Europe.

If study, in Jewish tradition, is the highest good it is never good enough in itself. One was expected to marry, and if possible to marry young. Father was a pious young man, industrious, good-looking with a graceful presence, and in due course a *shidduch* [love-match] was arranged for him and he married the pretty, vivacious daughter of a Vitebsk corn and flax merchant. As was usual in such matters Father would either have been supported as a scholar all his life or he would have entered his father-in-law's business, but the Russian Revolution came, the business was no more, and Father had to do something for which fate had left him wholly unequipped – make a living.

My mother ... was a handsome woman, with large, clear grey eyes and a self-consciously dignified bearing, as if determined not to be borne down by her lowly circumstances, and always kept us and herself in mind of her patrician origins. She was haughty and snobbish, yet lively and had a forceful way of expressing herself both in the things she said and the way she said them. Father by comparison seemed like a dormouse who had been roused from his sleep.

119

The wars and revolutions, the general chaos, ruined a great many families and many *yeshiva* [seminary] students who had been equipped for a life of prayer, contemplation and study, and who had been supported by their parents or in-laws, suddenly had to fend for themselves. My father's position, however, was not quite desperate, for my grandparents managed to scratch together sufficient funds to set him up with a shop in Breslev as a dealer in suiting materials. However, Father had a mildly pagan streak, which I have inherited in enlarged form, and loved the countryside; if business was slack and the weather was fine, he closed the shop and went out for a walk – which made the business even slacker. He also adhered to the Talmudic precept that one must trust men unless one has cause to distrust them, which was all right for sermons but not for business, and he was soon ruined.

By then he was the father of three or four children. He had been ordained as a rabbi shortly before his marriage, but so had a hundred thousand other Talmudical students. There was a Jewish tradition that one should not make a living from the Torah, but what was perhaps more immediately relevant was the fact that there was no living to be had from it. The towns and villages of Eastern Europe were teeming with Talmudists laden with learning, but without visible or, indeed, invisible means of support. 'He who does not teach his son a trade', said the Talmud, 'teaches him to steal', but the only trade for which Father and his contemporaries had been trained was that of sons-in-law and that, for the time being, was no longer a profitable calling. He had to find himself a craft, and after a couple of years' training he became a *shochet*, which has a certain amount of prestige as a semi-ecclesiastical profession and because it requires a considerable degree of learning. But it is as degrading and unpleasant an occupation as a man could have, for a *shochet*, not to put too fine a point on it, is a butcher, by which I do not mean a purveyor of slaughtered meat, but a slaughterer: literally, a professional cut-throat.

Father would never have been invited to Barovke had he been merely a rabbi, for Barovke could have done without religious ministration, but it could not do without kosher meat. He thus lived by the knife, but thought of himself only as a rabbi. There were two synagogues in the village and he ministered to both. He was, as the village policeman put it, the *Patushka*, the little father, of Barovke, and he gloried in the role.

Barovke was a mixed-up place. The area had been colonized by demobilized Russian soldiers after the Napoleonic wars and the peasantry, in so far as they said anything at all – for they were a dour lot – spoke Russian; the Jews spoke Yiddish; the intelligentsia, German. Who then spoke Latvian? Those whose jobs depended on it: postmasters, schoolmasters, government officials; in short, those who were paid to do so, for anyone in government service was well paid, or at least regularly paid, which is more than can be said of almost everyone else in Latvia. The old, which is to say the Russian, name for our village was Barovke; the new, or Latvian name, was Silene, and in school it was a punishable offence to call it anything else, though one was as likely to call Barovke Silene as one is to call Dublin, Baile Atha Cliath.

The Jews never spoke of the place as anything other than Barovke, not out of stubborn loyalty to old Russia, but because it sounded right; it was the sort of name Shalom Aleichem might have made up, like Kastrilovke or Anatevke, for 'Ke' in Yiddish suggests something small and beloved, and the final syllable conveyed something of its humble size and station. It was a clearing in the forest near the Latvian–Polish border, and one suspects that it came into existence in the first place because of the smuggling opportunities afforded by the border. It consisted of a few dozen shops and houses, some neatly grouped round the small cobbled square, the rest scattered in all directions, as if sown by the wind. They were built on high stone foundations to keep the timber above the level of the snows, with steep roofs and sagging windows, like unhappy eyes in an unhappy face. Doors too sagged, as did shutters, and there was a built-in lop-sidedness about the whole place. The more prosperous homes were brightly painted in red and yellow with white window frames. Many dwellings were set in small gardens or orchards, surrounded by an affected, tiny, brightly painted wooden fence, with the tops carved like the onion domes of a Russian church. No one in Barovke was so poor as not to have a fruit tree to his abode. Chickens scratched around in the streets, in the gardens and courtyards, and at mealtimes pecked around under the tables in the homes, sometimes fighting for the available provender with the cats. I do not know if anyone actually kept a cat, but cats insinuated their way into every household. On the other hand there was no Jewish home with a dog. Dogs – large, gruff, shaggy, snarling creatures – were something one associated with *goyim*. One fled at the sight of a dog, and to this day I am still inclined to cross over to the other side of the road at the sight of a poodle.

Barovke itself was – or so I thought – solidly Jewish, but as one grew older one became aware of another, posher, Barovke beyond, with more substantial buildings, some of them of brick rather than timber, built in regular rows, in neat streets with neat gardens. This other Barovke contained the occasional non-Jewish Jew, but it was otherwise as *Judenrein* [Jew-free] as Barovke proper was *goyimrein* [free of non-Jews].

The local doctor, dentist, apothecary and lawyer were all Jewish, but they were not, strictly speaking, part of the community. They went about their work bare-headed; one did not see them in synagogue; they worked and travelled on the Sabbath; it was doubtful whether they ate kosher (it was almost certain they did not), but no one was troubled by the fact, not even Father. They were university-trained and such people were not expected to be observant. One was, indeed, mildly reassured that they remained Jewish at all, and one felt flattered on the rare occasions that they graced the synagogue with their presence. They wore black Homburgs, instead of the cloth-caps worn by everyone else except Father; they wore ties; their jackets matched their trousers. They were the local gentry, save that, with the exception of the lawyer, Abrasha Pinkashovitz, they assumed no position of leadership in the community. Their contacts with it were purely professional. They descended, prescribed, took their money and returned to the elevated universe from whence they came. Father, who prepared some of their sons for the Barmitzvah, would return from their homes full of wonder. Telephones! Velvet curtains! English furniture! Carpets on the floor! But they must have held a lowly place in their professions to have got no further than Barovke. The first car in the neighbourhood was owned by the husband of the local midwife who seemed to spend his entire day in, on, or about the car. Perhaps it didn't have an engine, or perhaps he couldn't afford petrol, for I never saw him drive it. The second was owned by

Abrasha Pinkashovitz. The doctor, a pale-faced man with rimless glasses, who looked as if he was in need of a cure himself, went about his work on foot.

Father, for a rabbi of his school, was a progressive and enlightened figure, though he would have denied any such label, but as in most Orthodox Jewish families it was the womenfolk who exposed one to the modern world. Father had a substantial library, but with never a volume devoted to anything other than Holy Writ. There were the basic books themselves, the commentaries on them, commentaries on the commentaries, and commentaries on ... whereas my mother and sisters read profane literature in several languages, and I was seven or eight before it dawned upon me that not everything in print had been dictated by God to Moses on Mount Sinai. I was aware that people wrote letters to each other, but it was something of a revelation to discover that books could be the product of mortals, some of them, like Pushkin, Dostoevsky, Tolstoy, who were not even Jewish.

'Do you mean,' I asked, 'that you can write a book and people will pay you to read it?'

'Yes,' said Mother, 'if they like it.'

And I got myself a pencil and paper and began: 'Once upon a time there lived an old woman who never died ...' It was inspired by the sight of an old woman who had lived in Barovke and who was recalled even by the village ancients as being old when they were born. She was bent double with age and was said to be a hundred and seven.

The fact that Latvian Jewry was drawn to German culture made them suspect in Russian eyes and shortly after the outbreak of the First World War many Jews – including my father's family who were anything but Germanized – were deported into the interior. There then followed years of turmoil and terror, not unlike those experienced by Mother's family except that my father's parents went penniless into the war and came penniless out of it. In 1915 the Germans occupied Latvia. They pulled out in 1918 and in November of that year an independent Latvian republic was proclaimed, which was almost immediately threatened by a Bolshevik and then a German invasion, and it was not until 1920 that the Latvians were finally masters of their own country. There then followed a period which many Jews spoke of as *'die golderne yorn'* – the golden years. Jews, in common with other minorities, enjoyed and were encouraged to enjoy, cultural autonomy. There was a network of Jewish schools which formed part of the state system and which offered a choice of education in Russian, German and Yiddish. There was a Hebrew teachers' seminary, a Jewish music conservatoire, a Yiddish theatre, a flourishing Jewish press. Then in May 1934 – about a year after we settled in Latvia – there came a fascist coup under Karlis Ulmanis. Cultural pluralism was abandoned in favour of a policy of rigorous Latvianization. All the Jewish schools were closed except the religious ones, and they were placed under the control of the Agudah, a right-wing ultra-religious party. The non-Jewish schools had classes on Saturday from which many Jewish children had in the past been excused. Saturday attendance was now made compulsory, and Barovke was particularly affected, for it did not have the alternative of a Jewish state school, and Father protested that Jewish children were being compelled to desecrate their Sabbath.

It is difficult perhaps for the Western reader to appreciate the petulant temper of East European authority, and the protest must have involved Father in a prodigious, indeed reckless, display of courage, for apart from his natural timidity, he was in an exposed and vulnerable situation. Though he was born in Latvia he did not happen to be living there when the state was proclaimed and as far as the authorities were concerned he was a Russian, a Polack – possibly even a Red – but at all events a foreigner, and a Jewish foreigner at that. The headmaster of the school, a dapper little dried-up, yellowish being, like a Chinese ivory figurine, with a huge bald head, no eyebrows, and blue lips, was the local representative of the ruling party, the Gauleiter, so to speak, of Barovke, and he made the protest known to his superiors. An obscure rabbi – and he an alien – in an obscure village was questioning the authority of the state. Word went forth that Barovke should be rid of its meddlesome priest. And Father, by now comfortably established in a small house with a red roof and green shutters, set among cherry trees, with two daughters at school and a son approaching school age, and a fourth child still in early infancy, was served with an expulsion order. For the first time in his life he had known something like economic security. His position as Rabbi carried prestige but no salary, but as a *shochet* he charged so much per head per animal slaughtered. There were slack weeks in the summer and winter, and frantically busy ones on the approaches to the festivals, but overall he was able to earn an average of about one pound a week, which, though it offered no luxuries, meant that none of us went hungry, ragged or cold. Now, his humble sufficiency threatened, he turned for help to one Mordechai Dubin, the Agudah leader.

The Agudah was founded in 1912 to combat the inroads which Zionism was making into Jewish life, and it represented a type of Orthodoxy which was too rigid and extreme even for my father – who was, in any case, a lifelong Zionist – but it was favoured by the fascists as a pliable and submissive partner. The Kingdom to which it aspired was not of this world. What others demanded as of right, the Agudah was prepared to seek as a favour. Mordechai Dubin, head of the party, was a personal friend of Karlis Ulmanis. Many Jews regarded the cringing unctious attitude of the Agudah with bitterness and contempt, but many others believed that they owed their lives to the intercession of Dubin with higher authority – and my father was among them. The expulsion order was rescinded. But his troubles were not over, for his labour permit, without which he could not function as a *shochet*, was not renewed, and there all of Dubin's influence proved unavailing.

We were not left entirely destitute. Father could still pick up the odd shilling from private tuition. It was illegal for him to ply his trade and illegal for butchers to employ him, but he was still brought an occasional chicken to slaughter (which he killed in the backyard) and, with the assurance that the policeman next door would keep a blind eye to his movements, he darted down to the abattoir with his knives under his jacket, despatched a few sheep, and sneaked back, and in this way he was able to earn something like six to seven shillings a week which was just about enough to survive on in Barovke in 1936.

There is an old Yiddish saying that you shouldn't have to get used to what you can get used to (it sounds better in Yiddish), and we got used to it. We subsisted on herrings and black bread during the week, and somehow managed to eat reasonably well on the Sabbath and festivals, with white bread on the table and stuffed pike, and Mother's invariable compote of stewed prunes. We might have continued like that for years, but if one can get used to poverty, Father could not get used to his furtive existence. He felt like a hunted criminal and was beginning to crack under the strain. Finally, he found a job in Glasgow.

Exile

Throughout those harassing years many, perhaps most, East European Jews had two sources of comfort: their God in heaven and/or an uncle in America. (In the event, the latter sometimes proved more useful than the former.) Mother did not have an uncle in America, but she had one in Britain, which we thought of as an offshore island of America, and was therefore almost as good. Nor was he an ordinary uncle. He was, it was said, not only prosperous – which was the least one could expect of a relative in the West – he was a JP, a Justice of the Peace, which was translated to us simply as a Judge. Nay, a JUDGE! In every Jewish community there was a Beth Din, a rabbinical court, which dealt mainly with religious matters but to which Jews often resorted for arbitration. Father, as a rabbi, had served on such a court on innumerable occasions and could thus be considered a judge of sorts. But this distant uncle, Louis Daets by name, functioned on a more exalted plane and dispensed justice to *goyim*, and in our imagination he flourished as a veritable Solomon. We received cuttings about him from the Yiddish press, which were passed along the pews in synagogue, in the English-language Jewish press and even – so far had his fame spread – in the English language *goyish* press.

He was a distinguished-looking man with a fine head of hair, piercing, rather stern grey eyes, like my mother's, a formidable nose, an Edwardian moustache and beard, an Edwardian wing-collar and cravat, replete with pearl tie-pin, and a gold watch and chain with a pendant medal across a substantial stomach. The most impressive thing about the portrait was the beard. Barovke was full of beards, but they were wild, shaggy outcrops with a will and vigour of their own. This beard was cultivated, tamed, contained, as if every particular hair had been individually laid in place. He looked every inch the judge. Such an uncle was good as money in the bank, and it was to him that we finally turned when things in Barovke became impossible.

It so happened that there was a vacancy for a *shochet* in Glasgow, and Uncle, who apart from his other duties, was Chairman of the Board of Shechita (he was Chairman of the Board of almost everything else), offered Father a job. From then events followed in rapid succession. It was decided that Father would go to Glasgow (borrowing the necessary fare from Uncle) and would send for us as soon as he had saved enough for the tickets, which might take a year. In the meantime, my eldest sister, who had finished elementary school in Barovke, would go to a gymnasium in Dvinsk (or Daugapils, as it was known in Latvian, or Dunabourg in German), I would be sent to Breslev and my other sisters would remain in Barovke with my mother.

There was a great family reunion before Father left, and relatives came by the wagon-load from Breslev, Dvinsk and nearby Kreslavka. I don't know where they could all have slept, for our house had only three rooms of which but two were bedrooms – though in Jewish homes in those days … every room, including the kitchen, could be made to serve as a bedroom. (There was no inn in Barovke and important guests usually stayed with us, usually in my room, sometimes in my bed. There was a small man with a great bushy beard, a charity collector, who often slept in my bed, and who farted with such force that I was almost blasted out of bed.) And finally there was a great public dinner at which all of Barovke was present. I don't know what there was to eat or drink, but the speeches were many and endless. I came and went several times, but whenever I returned there was always someone on his feet paying tribute to my father, all genuinely meant and some delivered with tears. I remember in particular an elderly bearded figure called Simshon Ber, not for what he said, but because the tears he shed did not penetrate his beard but rolled down it like water off a duck's back and stained the tablecloth.

I left for Breslev some time before Father left for Glasgow and he accompanied me on foot as far as the Polish border (there was room beside me on the open cart, but he wanted to save the fare). It was a blazing hot day and he kept removing his Homburg and wiping his hatband and forehead. The horse was plodding slowly along the dry, rutted track and I kept dropping off to sleep. Father and I never had much to say to each other, especially when we had much to say, and were, I think, rendered inarticulate by affection. When we reached the border Father blessed me, but we did not kiss or cry, for we have always been afraid, or reluctant, perhaps even unable, to show emotion in our family, and to that extent we were Englishmen ready-made, except that I have sometimes felt – unjustifiably as I discovered – that Englishmen have no emotions to show.

I was six and about to receive my first bitter taste of exile. I stayed with my mother's family. They had been prosperous corn and flax merchants before the First World War, but had lost everything in the Russian Revolution. To my unsubtle mind people who lost everything were left with nothing, but instead I found people of substance who seemed better off in the depths of their penury than my father at the height of his prosperity.

There were two Breslevs, the old and the new, with the latter, which was also known as the Domques, built on high ground overlooking the former. Old Breslev was of timber, the new of stone. New Breslev had electricity, the old had none. Old Breslev was entirely Jewish, the new, entirely Polish, and any non-Jewish Jews who happened to be there kept quiet about their antecedents or were practising Christians. My grandfather's house was one of the largest in old Breslev, a two-storey affair, solidly built, with out-houses and a large, cobbled courtyard. The house seemed to be the general meeting place of everyone in Breslev. A constant whirl of figures, young and old, passed through it, and although one was always surrounded by people I never had any company or friends. My main source of delight was the cellar, a large dark place, which extended under the entire area of the house.

I have often wondered why I was so unhappy in Poland and the most obvious reason was that I was so happy in Latvia. In Barovke, first of all, I was at home. We were, in retrospect, poor, but who was not? One might have had regular meals only on the Sabbath, but one rarely went hungry the rest of the week and everyone in Barovke ate reasonably well in season. There were eggs in plenty in the spring and summer, fruit in plenty in the summer and autumn, and there was bread and milk at other times of the year, and if one waned in winter one waxed in the summer.

Then Barovke itself, and its surroundings, were a constant source of joy. There was a small lake at one end of the village and a large lake at the other, with a blithe, silvery, chuckling stream linking the two, and in the hot summer we were hardly out of the water, wading, swimming, fishing (darting by hand after the tiddlers who sought refuge under the stones). In the winter, muffled up like Eskimos, we went skating, sledging, skiing. It was a free, open life and an important part of the openness and freedom was the fact that the *goyim* were friendly: in Poland they were not.

Antisemit (with the accent on the last syllable) was an expression with which the Jewish child in Eastern Europe became familiar early in life. It entered into adult conversation a hundred times a day and in every possible context, and one took it to be one of the ills of life, like rheumatism, which was more painful at some time than others, but which one learned to live with. All *goyim* were presumed to be *antisemitten* unless they showed definite proof to the contrary, whereupon they were pronounced *Judenfreint* – philo-Semites. Thus, for example, Patushka, or 'little father' as the local Russian Orthodox priest was known, was a *Judenfreint*, as was the village policeman, a mild-mannered little man, with a Hitler moustache and a woebegone expression. Patushka sometimes played chess with my father, to whom he had an uncanny resemblance. They were both bearded and (in winter) both wore the same tall fur hats. They also both liked a schnaps, though Father was a Sabbath and festival drinker, whereas the Patushka packed a flask in his canonicals and was inclined to swig at it any time. He also, it was said, kept two concubines which, as Father observed, was perhaps easier than keeping one wife.

On market days Barovke was flooded with peasants and some of the small boys tried to provoke me by putting their forefingers together in a cross and kissing it – totally without effect, for I thought they were indulging in some sort of religious ritual. In short, given my limited experience, Barovke *goyim* were *Judenfreint*.

In Breslev, however, they all seemed to be *antisemitten* and, again, given my limited experience, they all were. I did not make one friend or acquaintance during that year in Breslev and wandered by myself from one end of the town to the other, up and down the main road and into the sideways. One day I wandered beyond the town and into the countryside when I saw two boys, a little older than me, sitting on the fence and regarding my approach with less than friendly interest. I looked at them, and they looked at me and I turned about with as much dignity as I could muster and began to walk back, breaking into a trot when I heard their steps behind me. They were upon me in a minute, knocked me to the ground and set about me with boot and fist. When I reached home battered and bleeding my grandmother turned on me. Idiot! Didn't I know it was dangerous to go beyond Breslev on my own? And of course I didn't. In Barovke one had been safe to roam at will. I had heard of Jewish persecutors as part of distant or not so distant history, but otherwise thought of anti-Semitism as a mere matter of sentiment: that some people disliked Jews much as others disliked, say, borsch. It had never occurred to me that one could still be knocked down, kicked and beaten just for being Jewish.

A few months after I went to Poland my father set out for Scotland, and after about a year he had saved up enough money to send us tickets to join him. My exile was about to come to an end.

I rejoined my mother and sister in Barovke to prepare for our emigration and found their position already transformed. Father was sending us £10 a month and we were rich, and one obvious sign of it was the succession of *meshulochim*, charity collectors, who can smell money as instinctively as bears smell honey, and who almost laid siege to our house. There were people in Barovke who earned more, but their income came in erratic lumps, and even when the going was good they were afraid to spend it in case it should go bad, whereas Father's two fivers in their registered envelope came as assuredly as day followed night. British banknotes now look much like any other currency and are usually worth less, but there was a grave dignity to those large white flimsy fivers with their glossy black print and their whirly figures; they looked as if they had been painted by hand. Framed they would have looked like a college diploma.

The fact that for the first time since the Russian Revolution Mother was again in funds did little to change her way of life, for though she was from a rich family and Father from a poor one, she was rather better at husbanding cash; but it did mean that Anna, an old, battered Russian *babushka*, who used to come in as a home-help in the not infrequent occasions when Mother was ill, now came every day. She was a chain-smoker and rolled her own cigarettes from any paper to hand – usually newspaper. She once picked up one of the fivers and began to fill it with tobacco, when Mother snatched it from her grasp.

We became very attached to Anna and went to see her before we left Barovke. She lived in a thatched hovel in the woods which, in an English setting, would have been picturesque, but which to our eyes summed up all that was dreadful in poverty. She was a typical Russian peasant woman: stoic, hardy, tireless, uncomplaining. She clasped us all to her great bosom before we left – I still remember the smell of stale tobacco – and drenched us with tears.

In the meantime we were hearing wondrous things about Glasgow: its magnificence, its towering buildings, its size, its open spaces, its wealth. People, wrote Father, ate four meals a day whether they were hungry or not, and that at set times – breakfast at eight, lunch at one, tea at five and supper at seven. In Barovke one had a cup of tea and a bun at breakfast and *varmess* – a warm meal – towards evening, but otherwise one snatched a bite whenever one was hungry – provided always there was a bite to snatch. In Glasgow, doctors, 'and even professors', attended synagogue religiously every Sabbath, which made us feel it was a holy city. In Glasgow we learned, 'great Jewish merchants' kept their shops shut on Shabbat, whereas in Latvia (there were no millionaires in Barovke itself) anyone beyond a certain level of prosperity could, so to speak, arrange his own terms with the Almighty and did not keep – and was not expected to keep – the Sabbath. And – most wondrous of all – the *goyim* were friendly. Elsewhere one presumed *goyim* were unfriendly unless they showed proof to the contrary. In Glasgow, wrote Father, it was the other way about, they were *all* friendly – 'even the *beitzimer'* (lower-class non-Jew).

The only non-Jews with whom Father had any contact were our immediate neighbours (whom he would greet with: 'Good morning, nice day', whatever the state of the weather), and Irish pluckers in the poultry slaughter house in the Gorbals. So much of the little English that he knew he acquired from an English translation of the Talmud (which he used as a sort of introduction to the English language), and from the Irish pluckers, and some of the expressions he picked up sounded odd in his mouth. Thus, he referred to Mother, whose superior airs would humble a duchess, as 'the missus'. A famous rabbi once lay dying in a Glasgow hospital and Father was among the privileged few to be admitted to his bedside. 'How is he?' he was asked as he emerged, and Father shook his head gravely: 'He's a goner', he said.

If the Scots *goyim* were friendly I am not sure whether the Latvian ones were unfriendly and certainly I met no one in Scotland as kindly and affectionate as old Anna. The only actual, card-carrying Latvian anti-Semite I had heard of was Tolk – splendid name for a villain – a border policeman who had shot and killed a Jew trying to smuggle himself over the frontier, though I dare say he would have shot his own father trying to do the same thing. One certainly did not find in Latvia the atmosphere of brooding hatred one had experienced in Poland. The anti-Semitism which one did encounter was mainly institutional. Any Jew in Eastern Europe who sought to get anywhere could take it for granted that he would meet handicaps at every stage of his progress from which the non-Jew was free; whereas – according to Father – Britain was entirely opened to the talents. Secondary education was free and, if one worked hard enough and was bright enough, one could even get to university for nothing. All this was written, or at least read out to us by Mother, in a continuous tone of wonder and awe. 'Who knows,' she said to me 'you might even be a doctor.'

No one not brought up in Eastern Europe can appreciate the awe with which a doctor was regarded by Jew or non-Jew. If someone was so ill as to need a doctor – and he had to be very ill (for minor ailments one approached the apothecary) – the house was prepared for his coming. Beds were hurriedly made, jackets were donned to cover braces, the patient was tidied and cleaned and propped up, and when the great man entered everyone rose. One remained standing in his presence and addressed him in a hushed voice. If the patient died it was taken to be the work of God; if he survived at all, the praise of the doctor was sung about the neighbourhood; and if he was cured, he was spoken of in hushed tones as a miracle-worker. A doctor couldn't fail. My ambition at this time, however, was to be a rabbi which, in later years, I almost fulfilled.

'Mit a gutten Engils'

The first, and perhaps the greatest disappointment, was Father himself. I had looked forward to our reunion as a restoration of the close, cosy, intimate existence we had known before. Glasgow, as I had envisaged it, was to be Barovke plus regular meals, but nothing was the same any more and Father himself had changed. He had arrived in Glasgow a *heimisher* [homely] rabbi, and was pulled aside with advice – mainly from colleagues who had settled in Glasgow some years before – that he should adapt his appearance a little to his environment, and thus he removed the sidelocks which he used to have tucked in behind his ears, and trimmed his beard till it hardly covered his chin. I was later to feel embarrassed by the fact that he had a beard at all, but his flowing whiskers, with their reddish tinge, had been so much a part of his personality that I hardly recognized him without them.

In Barovke I used to accompany him through the mists and across the moist meadows to synagogue every morning. In Glasgow he could not attend synagogue on weekdays, for he had to be up about five to get to the slaughter-house at six (he travelled on an early-morning workman's ticket), so that my visits to synagogue – which in Barovke had formed the centre of my existence – were confined to evenings and weekends, and as time went on my evening visits also lapsed.

Provincial Jewish life in the 1930s was still in the hands of immigrants who, if only to establish their own bona fides as Englishmen, demanded one quality above all others from their rabbis, that they speak *'mit a gutten Engils'* – which was the one quality father lacked. He was a good man, a pious man, a learned man with a fine presence, a good rabbinical diploma, with recommendations from some of the greatest sages in Eastern Europe (written in a Hebrew which would have been Greek to most people in Glasgow), but of *'Engils'*, good or bad, he had none. He was, as far as Glasgow was concerned, not Rabbinic material, and thus for six days of the week he was a slaughterer and on the seventh day he was nobody, till towards the end of his life, when the sons of immigrants assumed the mantles of their fathers and became leaders of the community.

They spoke a '*gutten Engils*' themselves and were thus not concerned about the Englishness of their clergy, and Father became rabbi of an almost defunct congregation in the Gorbals. By then he had mastered the language sufficiently to attempt a sermon in English, though most people who came to hear him would have preferred him to speak in Yiddish. In Yiddish he had sufficient power of oratory almost to penetrate the language barrier, but when he turned to English all his natural facility for words was lost. He would put together his thoughts with the help of the collected works of English rabbis whose sermons were a patchwork of platitudes couched in clichés.

Glasgow was a hard-headed and, in some ways, a hard-faced, workaday place where material advancement was as a rule given priority over everything else, and the city itself was in many ways a monument to this creed. With its river and hills it has a natural setting as splendid as Athens or Rome, but for over a century it has been at the mercy of speculative builders, railway developers, industrialists, who were allowed to darken every prospect provided they could make tuppence grow where a penny grew before. But with all that, possibly because so sombre a place on earth commends to the mind the heavens, it was in those days a very religious city, not in the sense that it was particularly pious – that Glasgow has never claimed for itself – but because religion exercised the imagination and the energies of a large part of the population (though not always to the extent of affecting its ways), and with it came a considerable deference to the clergy.

Jewish clergymen in those days used to be clad by Church outfitters from head to foot, including even the dog-collar, and they found that people would offer them seats in the tram, bank managers extended them credit on liberal terms, policemen touched their helmets in salutation.

Glasgow Jewry, on the other hand, had scant deference for the cloth. The elders were shopkeepers, warehousemen, dealers and traders of various sorts who had made a bit of money, and gave a bit away, and who in their struggle for a livelihood had forgotten any Jewish knowledge they may have possessed without acquiring any compensating knowledge from the outside. You were somebody or nobody according to how much you were worth and, to an extent, how much you gave, and if you were rich enough, you were sometimes even absolved from giving. Father, who had tended to view the community with excessive deference when he first came, came to regard it with excessive distaste towards the end of his life. He once said 'ten good men and true would have been sufficient to save Sodom, were there that many good men in Glasgow? There was Ellis Isaacs, and he's dead; Abraham Goldberg, and he's dead; Hirshow, and he's dead; Hyman Tankel, and he's dead; Eli Jacobs, and he's dead; Jack Mandel, and he's dead.'

He did not include Uncle who was by then in his eighties and still showing every sign of life.

Uncle was another of the disappointments of Glasgow. Instead of the JUDGE, the exalted personage sitting on high, dispensing justice to the multitudes, I found a sad little man with a drooping moustache, a baggy suit, soup-stained lapels and a large, eccentric wife in a large, yellow, moth-eaten fur, which she had never left off her shoulders summer or winter. Every time Aunt came on a visit I would rummage among the tufts to establish the origins of the fur, and it seemed to me that it was fashioned out of marmalade cats.

Both Uncle and Aunt spoke a broken English (Aunt knew hardly any English at all), which made me wonder what sort of judge Uncle could have been and I soon discovered that a Justice of the Peace did not have quite the exalted role I had imagined. He was from time to time required to take his turn on the local magistrate's bench. He did not understand much English, but he knew a drunk when he saw one (he rarely saw anyone else), and tended to mete out ten days to anyone who came before him, so that he became known as the Ten-Day Wonder. A growing number of stipendiary magistrates displaced more and more of the JPs whose role had become increasingly ornamental, but during the Second World War and the immediate postwar years, Uncle was kept busy by a succession of small boys who had lost their sweet-ration coupons and needed the signature of a JP on their application for new ones, which gave him a function of sorts. He once said: 'I've got the bad teeth of a whole generation on my conscience.'

Uncle and Aunt were first cousins, and had left Russia shortly after their marriage early in the century. They reached Glasgow *en route* for America, but Uncle found friends there and built up a thriving business as a credit draper, or 'tally-man', as they were known in Scotland, selling a pair of shoes here, a pair of trousers there, to the working-class areas of Glasgow, and was repaid at the rate of a penny or tuppence a week. They had two daughters both precociously bright and very beautiful, and after the First World War they set out with their children to visit their families in Poland. There, as Uncle put it, 'something unfortunate happened'. He never explained what the misfortune was, but Mother told us. A typhus epidemic was raging in Eastern Europe. Both children succumbed to it and died after a short illness. Uncle and Aunt had set out a young and happy couple with young children, and returned elderly and derelict.

Once they had lost their children they adopted the community as their family, and there was hardly a major Jewish organization of which Uncle was not President, Chairman or Treasurer, but his main joy was the Queen's Park Synagogue: a large red-sandstone building which stood, and still stands, near the River Cart on the south side of Glasgow. It was built largely through his efforts, and partly with his money, and he haunted the building at all times of the day and night.

There is in the centre of every Orthodox synagogue a *bimah*, or raised platform, from which the cantor leads the congregation in prayer, and in front of the *bimah* there is, like the quarter-deck of a ship, an area known as the Warden's Box, which accommodates the lay-leaders of the congregation in their panoply of striped trousers and top hats. Uncle was more in the box than out of it, partly because he almost owned it, but partly because no one else applied himself to the affairs of the congregation so completely. And he was a different man in the box, more erect, more assured. A new light shone in his eyes, there was an extra vigour to his voice. He looked like an elderly, if diminutive, lion.

The relationship between our families was not of the happiest. First of all, Mother could not forgive them for the fact that we had needed their help in the first place. Secondly she felt that they were patronizing us, which to an extent they were. They had taken it upon themselves to pull us into the twentieth century, and Mother suspected early in our sojourn that Uncle in his wing-collars and Aunt in her moth-eaten fur were possibly not themselves in the avant-garde of contemporary life. It was Aunt (though I may be doing her an injustice) who suggested that as a prospective Briton I could not go through life as Chaim Icyk Bermant, and therefore when I entered Battlefield School, in September 1938, I was registered as Hyman Berman and, understanding what was expected of me, I took the matter further. There was a Jewish boy upstairs from us with the name of Isaac, who was called Francis. Icyk is the Polish for Isaac and I therefore began signing myself Hyman Francis Berman, and I still have an exercise book with that name on the cover. Nobody of course ever called me Hyman or Francis and I was known variously as Hymie, Hi Hi, or Hei Ho, and even Haimish. At home I was called Chaim Icke and finally when I enrolled at Glasgow University I saw no reason for departing from the name on my birth certificate and reverted to Chaim Icyk Bermant. Chaim Icyk, moreover, means life and laughter in Hebrew, and although I have not always lived up to my names one can go through life with worse labels.

My own complaint against Uncle was that he was less than avuncular. The Yiddish (and Hebrew) for relatives is *krovim*, near ones, and in Eastern Europe they were literally just that. Their home was an extension of yours, yours of theirs. One came and went without invitation or bidding, dropped in for meals, raided the larder, and even among non-relatives one lived in a world of open doors, except, of course, last thing at night, when there came a heavy clanking of bolts and bars and the clatter of shutters. One of the first things that struck me about Glasgow was that doors stayed shut no matter how hard one pushed, and that one had to pull or push a bell, or knock to be admitted. The bells were great fun and for the first week or so after we moved in I was a source of harassment to the entire neighbourhood and beyond, but I could not get over the fact that doors were locked in broad daylight, even when people were at home, and there was no door more thoroughly locked than Uncle's.

If we were disappointed with Uncle and Aunt, they were more than disappointed with us. They would, I think have liked to adopt us as their second family, but Mother was too prickly, and we remained too stubbornly alien, or to use an expression which echoed about our ears almost endlessly for our first year in Glasgow, we were incorrigible 'greeners'. Other newcomers had arrived in Glasgow at about the same time and had built flourishing businesses. They spoke reasonable English, were fashionably dressed, kept open house and could make polite conversation; whereas for a long time we looked and dressed and spoke and behaved as if we had just stepped off the immigrant boat, and on those rare occasions when we were invited anywhere we sat together in an awkward, silent huddle. It was not for want of trying to adapt ourselves to our surroundings. Father had already sacrificed three-quarters of his beard. Mother, who had arrived in a voluminous, ankle-length fur coat and cape, of the type necessary to carry one through a Russian winter, had remodelled it till it stopped short of the calf. My sisters, who had long plaits running halfway down their backs, had hair-cuts, and I, who arrived cropped as a convict, allowed my hair to grow till it was long enough for a parting. Moreover, my mother and sisters went to night-school to learn English, while my father struggled with huge chunks of the English translation of the Talmud. But it was all unavailing. We were different and felt different and were deeply, in fact excessively, conscious of the fact that we were 'greeners'.

There were several refugees among my contemporaries at school, among them a little pink-faced chap with rimless glasses whom I called The Professor. When he enunciated a word of English, he did so exercising every muscle in his face, so that every syllable stood out in relief. In the lavatory one morning I noticed that he had a long, drooping foreskin to his little member, like an overlong sleeve – more foreskin than member in fact. I did a double-take, and it was still there, but to make trebly sure I followed him round until he had to go again, and there was no mistaking that he had an appendage which, given his race, shouldn't have been there. And he made no attempt to hide it, and indeed when he had completed his business swung it around with something like defiance. I could no more conceive of a Jew with a foreskin than of an elephant without a trunk, and for a long time I wondered if I should denounce him as an imposter.

There was a special class for foreign pupils taken by a tall, distinguished-looking, silver-haired woman, called Agnes Smith (the Scottish boys called her Big Aggie), who had an exotic line in spats which came right up to her finely moulded calves. She taught us in German, which I, with my knowledge of Yiddish, was able to follow. Within a month the refugee children were

138

out of the special class and in amongst the others, while I had Big Aggie all to myself till the end of term.

Uncle and Liebe Sheine were not our only guides to British life and civilization. Neighbours, colleagues, friends, all chipped in with their bits of counsel and though we eagerly took instruction from every quarter we tended to lapse into our alien ways. Father had to visit some important communal figure one evening. When he wasn't back by ten, Mother was a little concerned. When eleven o'clock struck and he was still not home she was almost frantic. By eleven-thirty she was on the point of calling the police (she would have called them if we had had a phone), when he came staggering in, white with exhaustion. 'I only intended to stay a few minutes', he explained, 'but every time I rose to leave, they kept asking me if I couldn't stay, so what could I do? I stayed.'

Similarly, when people stopped to ask Mother how she was, she would tell them, and as she was rarely in anything but indifferent health, she had a lot to tell.

We were lavishly entertained one evening by a distant relative who said that now we had got to know each other we should see each other more and that we should treat his home as ours. I took him at his word and was round there early the following morning. He met me at the gate, and without even enquiring whether I had money for the fare (which I hadn't), propelled me on to the first tram.

Some years later Father said that the first thing to learn about the English was that they don't say what they mean and don't mean what they say, and we compiled a private family glossary of English words and phrases together with their true meaning, such as:

'How are you?' (I'm not interested.)
'You must come in and see us.' (Keep your distance.)
'Make yourself at home.' (Keep your grubby hands off the furniture.)
'Do have another.' (Haven't you had enough?)
'Do stay.' (Are we never going to get rid of you?)
'How nice to see you!' (What, you here again?)
'That was a lovely evening.' (Yawn.)
'You've got such lovely children.' (What horrible ruffians.)

'You must come again.' (That's the last we've seen of you –
I hope.)
'You shouldn't have bothered.' (Is that the best you can
do?)

Back home in Breslev and Barovke there was a tradition of *vos
afen lung, dos afen tzung* (what's on the lung, that's on the
tongue). The tactful went so far as keeping their mouth shut, but
words were approached with a certain deference, and to have
used them in such a way as to reverse or obscure their meaning
would have been regarded as a form of sacrilege. It took us a
long time to come to terms with English civility.

Glasgow, my Glasgow

I found the size and scale of Glasgow bewildering. I was warned
that it would be big, 'twice the size of Riga', wrote Father. I had
been to Riga and it was certainly big, but it was open and leafy,
and one did not have to move far from the city centre to see
fields beyond the end of the road, whereas there was something
infinite about Glasgow. One moved beyond one street to find
another and beyond that more streets, and beyond that still
more, with four-storeyed tenements on every side like dark ram-
parts. After Barovke with its great open skies, its lakes and rivers,
woods and meadows, one felt imprisoned.

Our first address was the Gorbals where Father had lodgings
with distant relatives, and the Gorbals, somehow, was less intim-
idating than other parts of the town for it reminded me vaguely
of Dvinsk. There were Yiddish posters on the hoardings,
Hebrew lettering on the shops, Jewish names, Jewish faces,
Jewish butchers, Jewish bakers with Jewish bread, and Jewish
grocers with barrels of herring in the doorway. The herrings in
particular brought a strong whiff of home. One heard Yiddish in
the streets – more so, in fact, than English – and one encoun-
tered figures who would not have been out of place in Barovke.
It was only when we moved into our flat in Battlefield Gardens
that I began to feel my exile, for Battlefield – the area was named
after the Battle of Langside which took place on a nearby hill –

was, certainly in the late 1930s, posh, even elegant. In the Gorbals one ascended to one's flat up a dark stairway smelling of urine. In Battlefield all was light and cleanliness with a slight touch of Dettol in the air. The close, as the entrance to the flats was called, was lined with cream and green tiles; there was a large window on every landing which looked out on a small back-green (soon to be occupied by a large air-raid shelter). The buildings, four storeys high and faced with grey granite, were flanked by small privet hedges and ornamental cast-iron railings, and they looked out on a small garden ringed with trees. No one had access to the garden, not even the surrounding tenants, for it was fenced in and it was only when the landlord could not any longer afford the upkeep of the gardens, that the railings gradually fell away and it came to resemble a bomb-site with a small jungle of tall grass and wild flowers. Our flat, with its large kitchen, hall-way, two bedrooms and lounge (or 'big room' as we called it), was palatial compared to anything we had known previously (and in actual cubic feet of air space – for the rooms were all lofty – compared well with anything I have known since), but it was on the first floor, and it was an odd sensation to go out of one's front door and not find grass under one's feet. One was, so to speak, suspended above ground. The garden was there to be seen but not used. There were no trees to which one could tie a hammock, or in whose shade one could sit on hot afternoons. There was no ground on which to play or picnic. I kept searching for the country beyond Glasgow like a cat trying to sniff its way back to its abode, and for a while I thought I had found it: I had chanced upon a park.

The parks are the glory of Glasgow. They are numerous, large, varied in character and not too tamed, and I doubt if there is a city of similar size in Europe so richly provided with open spaces (and with such easy access to more), but the first park I approached – it was Queens Park – was enclosed behind tall, pointed, cast-iron railings with huge, ornamental gates and I thought I had perhaps stumbled upon some great private estate. I ventured in with some hesitancy, but no one threw me out and the park became my playground.

The second redeeming feature of Glasgow was the trams. They were large and ungainly, and rounded corners with sparks flying in all directions and a screeching like souls in torment, but seen from a distance, before their loud clatter assailed the ears, they had the majesty of galleons in full sail. Different colours indicated different destinations. The red tram went to Milngavie, the yellow to Anniesland, the green to Renfrew Ferry, the blue to Rutherglen, the white to Oatlands. If there was a black tram I should imagine it went to the cemetery, but I do not remember one. The colour code must have been a boon to the illiterate, but a handicap to the colour-blind. It was my impression that the green, blue and white trams went to the rougher neighbourhoods, and the yellow and red to the more elegant ones. When they introduced the Coronation tram, a slimmer, trimmer, streamlined version of the old model, they painted it in the beautiful cream, gold and green livery of the city, but it was confined at first to the posh Bellahouston–Pollokshields–University run.

The third redeeming feature, and the one which finally reconciled me to Glasgow, was the library. I was not at first aware that one could actually take books out of the library (and that without paying), it was privilege enough to be able to read them. For a few months, until I knew sufficient English, I spent my time poring over pictures, but as I graduated to words I became a Beatrix Potter addict. I was nearly nine then and rather old for such literature (except that one is never too old for Beatrix Potter), but among the animals, the mice, the moles, the toads, the squirrels, the ducks, I rediscovered something of Barovke. Our house had never harboured an animal other than a cat, and the cat was less pet than mouse-trap. We also had a hen or two, with whom it was difficult to establish any lasting relationship. But to an extent the whole of Barovke and its surroundings were part of our demesne and it was alive with rabbits, squirrels, moles, mice, toads and other Potterish characters, and on hot afternoons, when the village slept, the ducks almost took over Barovke.

If I was coming to enjoy Glasgow itself, I was finding less pleasure in Jewish Glasgow. I still went to synagogue every evening, but was beginning to find it a chore … and when I came to synagogue in the evenings I would find about a dozen middle-aged men sitting in small clusters about the large empty building chatting in low voices on the events of the day, and waiting for the service to begin. Beside them one might find five or six Yiddish-speaking elders, among them usually my uncle, who came out of habit and belief and who remained to study a page of the Talmud. There was no one there even remotely my age. I was regarded as the mascot and loaded with sweets and chocolates, and given cigarette cards, and even an occasional penny, but the bribes were not sufficient to ease the sense of desolation I felt in the large, cold, empty building. However, things cheered up on Friday evening.

... In Scotland in winter it begins to get dark between three and four o'clock in the afternoon, and Jewish boys were released from school an hour early to prepare themselves for Shabbat. Some boys promptly hived off to the pictures. (One local cinema, otherwise closed in the afternoon, was suspected of running special matinees for these delinquents.) But the more pious among us (and we were not that numerous) bathed and washed and changed and polished our boots and brushed our hair and rushed, smelling of Brylcreem and carbolic, self-conscious, semi-sacred figures, through the profane bustle of Friday evening shoppers, to synagogue.

One Friday afternoon, shortly after we had settled into Battlefield Gardens, I was sent out to buy a tin of boot-polish (or *chromaline* as it is known in Yiddish). I was by then sophisticated enough to appreciate that one probably could not get it in the Union Bank of Scotland, or the laundry, or the greengrocer, or the baker, or even the newsagent, but at Caskie's (... the outfitters) I stopped, and as I did not know how to describe my need in English, I explained what I wanted in mime.

'Ah,' said the brothers in unison, 'polish.' I stopped, nonplussed.

'No,' I said, 'Latvian.' Caskie's was later to assume a symbolic significance for me.

I was also becoming old enough to be troubled by events outside my own small, private world. This awareness had already been growing upon me in Barovke. People gathered in small knots outside the synagogue after service talking in low voices, with much shaking of heads and many sighs and consternation radiated from every side. Times were always troubled, but these times were more troubled than others, and a new figure had emerged to join Pharaoh, Amalek, Haman, Torquemada and other Jewish persecutors – Adolf Hitler. At this time, with his

Chaplin moustache, frenzied orations, wild eyes and preposterous salute, most Barovke boys found Hitler a vaguely comical
figure and we used to blacken our upper lips with charcoal and
go goose-stepping round Barovke *sieg-heiling* at the tops of our
voices. To the adults, however, he was no joke, and neither
indeed were we, and when we travelled though Germany, my
mother was petrified lest I should do one of my Hitler imper-
sonations.

In Glasgow people felt less directly threatened, but here too
the talk was all of Czechoslovakia, Danzig, Memel and – a con-
fusing expression – 'the Polish corridor'. Father acquired a large
radio shortly after we arrived and sat with his ear to the loud-
speaker twiddling dials and pressing knobs, catching the news
in whatever language it would emerge. He found English rather
hard to follow, but he understood German well, and could
derive some meaning from most Slavic languages, and the
whoops, whistles and whines of the radio, with the occasional
voice fading in and out of the noise dominated the late hours of
the night.

One evening we all trooped down to Battlefield school to be
fitted with gas-masks. For father this was a moment of crisis, for
in the event of a gas attack he could be smothered by his own
beard, and one of his colleagues suggested that he remove it
entirely except for a token presence of hair on the point of his
chin, but to have gone into the world virtually beardless in such
a situation would have been tantamount to a public declaration
of no confidence in the Almighty. He kept his beard and, as he
said to me after the war: ' You see, nothing happened.'

One Shabbat afternoon in late August there was a special celebration in the Queens Park Synagogue, and we received the
large, sugar-coated biscuits, the sweet wine and lemonade,
which were the usual part of a synagogue treat, plus Lyons ice-
creams which were particularly welcome on the hot afternoon.
Several of the elders of the congregation had forgone their
Shabbat afternoon sleep – no small act of self-denial – to be present, and several of them made speeches of such length that we
felt our ice-cream was well earned. Uncle, too, spoke. His voice
faltered several times and there were moments when I was
afraid he might break down. He lived for the weekly encounters
with the children. When the next Sabbath came there wouldn't

be a young face in the congregation, nor the sound of a young voice, not even mine. The town would be like Hamelin.

See You After Four

We rose early and found the hall full of baggage and the kitchen table full of sandwiches. My parents must have been up half the night. My eldest sister was away from home training to be a nurse and would shortly be joining the army nursing corps. The rest of us were to be evacuated. It was a word which I had heard a lot, but with whose implications I was still unfamiliar.

We were taken by taxi to St Enoch Station where we found about every child in Glasgow lined up with gas-mask case slung over his shoulder and a label dangling from him like a mailbag. It was all very orderly, though the excitement in the air gave an extra pungency to the smoke from the engine which enveloped the station. There were some tear-stained mothers, but few tear-stained children. Most of us felt as if we were about to embark on a prolonged treat and had, indeed, each been handed a large paper bag which contained among other things, one tin of bully beef, a tin of Carnation milk, a tin of Nestle's milk and chocolate caramel wafers. We could not wait to get on the train, and when it finally pulled out, our cheers nearly raised the glass roof of the station.

Our destination was Annan in Dumfriesshire, near the English border. My two sisters were billeted on a small farm on the edge of the town, and a large, freckle-faced boy with wavy hair, called Myer Tobias, and I were found billets in the village of Cummertrees, a few miles away.

It was a large house, set among trees behind a high wall. The rooms were large and lofty with tall windows, but light virtually excluded by curtains within and the trees without, and the place was full of dark corners and gloomy passages. In spite of the size of the house and the number of its rooms, its only inhabitants were a heavily built, semi-paralysed old man with a scarlet face so glossy as to be almost glazed, and a semi-paralysed old spaniel with eyes like running sores. They were looked after by a robust, red-faced woman with snow-white hair who, with rolled-up sleeves and formidable arms, seemed permanently braced for action. It was a summer's day, but there was a fire burning in the hearth. The old man sat on one side of the fire, the old dog snoozed by the other: a slight breeze moaned through the trees outside. We sat near the fire while the woman busied herself with tea. The old man looked at us, and we looked at him.

'Nice day,' I said. The old man grunted. The old dog snorted and twitched in his sleep. I had not felt so desolate since I left Barovke.

A few minutes later the woman pushed in the tea-trolley and I was startled out of my depression. I stemmed from a world of tea-drinkers, but tea back home was a matter of a glass of tea with lemon, or English tea, as we called it, with a bun or a biscuit or a slice of bread. But this was a wedding feast of a tea, thin slices of brown bread, slices of white bread, with butter and jam, and various bakemeats, with whose character I was unfamiliar, but which I later got to know as bannocks and crumpets and pancakes and scones and madeira cake and fruit cake and Swiss rolls. We did not get such a tea every day, but we did get it once a week, and the memory of the last treat with the anticipation of the next, carried us over the blank days in between. This was an aspect of British life of which no one had told me, and I came to cherish not only the tea but the whole aura of tea-time.

I was under the impression that one was expected to consume everything placed before one, which I did, and when I staggered upstairs to unpack, I sat down on my bed and fell asleep fully clothed.

I was away from parents, from familiar ways, but in a sense I had come home. A day or two later there was an incident which took me back beyond Barovke to Breslev.

Myer and I travelled to and from school by bus. One day after school, two or three local boys alighted from the bus and followed us. When we quickened our pace, they quickened theirs, and Myer, who was born in Glasgow and made of fairly stern stuff, stopped, turned round and asked what they wanted. I had no doubt at all what they wanted and grabbed my satchel tightly under my arm and ran. Together we might have given a good account of ourselves, separated we were, to use a Scottish expression, Amalakated. Two boys attacked Myer and bruised him about the head and body, the third caught up with me and gave me two black eyes and a swollen lip. But worse than the injuries were the memories they evoked. The *goyim* were not friendly after all, at least not in Annan. Added to which, Myer would not speak to me. I was yellow, he said. I had only lately come to terms with being a 'greener'. Being yellow was new to me. I presumed he meant I was a coward, which perhaps I was, though it seemed to me that to run when one is outnumbered – especially by boys older than oneself – seemed a perfectly natural, perhaps even a commendable thing to do. That night I wrote a long, tear-stained letter to my parents, demanding to be taken home. I was prepared to face the bombers and bombs; I could not face the anti-Semites.

When I got to school the next morning I found that Myer and I were not the only casualties. Half the school looked as if it had been involved in battle, which, indeed it had. There had been a concerted attack by the local boys against the evacuees – or 'Glasgow khillies' as they were known. My injuries were not incurred from the fact that I was Jewish, but that I was a town boy, a Glaswegian. It was the most reassuring revelation of my young life. I gloried in the name of Glaswegian, and have not ceased to glory in it since. I became visibly taller, more erect, more robust. I was attacked again, sometimes by myself, sometimes as part of a crowd, but no matter the odds, I always stood my ground and gave as good as I got, sometimes with compound interest. From a mere readiness to defend myself I moved close to assuming the Glaswegian pugnacity, and I had but to suffer the merest slight, sometimes only imagined, to retort with the standard invitation: 'See you after four.' I often came home with a bleeding nose or a mangled ear, but they were a small price to pay for the joys of battle.

I widened my circle of acquaintances and for the first time numbered *goyim* among my friends, including one small chap with glasses, lately down from an approved school, who kept stealing bicycles and bringing them to me. Several of the boys sometimes came home with me, but were made less than welcome by the housekeeper. She complained that their hobnail boots were ruining the carpets and marking the floor, and that they were disturbing the peace of the old man and his dog, though neither gave any signs of disturbance – nor, indeed, that they were aware of the outside world at all – but finally both for their sakes and mine, I was moved to another billet, nearer Annan. My host was Mr K – a young farmer with a large, fresh, pink face with dimpled cheeks, and two older sisters, maiden ladies, the one tall, the other short, who looked as if they might be religious, which, as I soon discovered, they were, and, what was worse, they took pains to make sure that I remained the same.

The sisters began their evening meal with a prayer, which seemed excessive for the fare that followed. They had their main meal at lunch-time and the evening meal, which they called high-tea, consisted of eggs with everything. On Monday it was poached eggs, on Tuesday fried, on Wednesday omelette, on Thursday scrambled. Sometimes by way of change we had a kipper or pilchards, but if we did I could never be quite sure what day it was.

The taller and older of the sisters, a mousey-haired woman with streaks of grey, and little blue veins showing through her cheeks, was hard of hearing. The brother, with his large cheerful face and white eyebrows, might utter something about that pig, or this cow, but otherwise had nothing to say, nor was I particularly talkative, so that conversation at table tended to be somewhat halting.

'And did you have a nice day, Hyman?' the older sister would begin brightly, and my reply was always the same:

'Yes.' And we would munch in silence for a time, then the brother might intrude with:

'Gladys is drying up.'

'Gladys?'

'Drying up.'

'She's drying up, Gladys is,' said the younger sister in a loud voice for the benefit of the older one.

'Is she due then, Arthur?'

'She's long past due.'

'She's what?'

'Long past due, Flora.'

'You needn't shout. I can hear.'

The high tea was the last meal of the day except for a mug of cocoa at bed-time. It occurred to me later that the reason why they confined themselves to a diet of eggs was to keep my fare kosher.

148

I was still of an age when I tended to measure the wealth of a family by the amount they ate and the hours they worked. The poor, it was generally known, or so it seemed to me, ate little and worked a lot. The Ks ate less well than we did in Glasgow (wartime shortages were to make themselves felt later), and worked harder than anyone I had ever met, and no matter how early I rose in the morning or how late I went to bed, they were always up and about - even on Sunday, and I sometimes wondered if they ever went to bed at all. And if they weren't busy in the house, they were busy in the cow-shed or the dairy, or the hen-house or the kitchen garden. And yet they showed signs of affluence. In Barovke if someone had a cow he was a man of property. The Ks had over a dozen cows in milk, and several heifers, and they farmed nearly a hundred acres of land. They also had a car, not much of one I admit, with spindly tyres, but it went, and Arthur used it to deliver his two sisters to church on Sunday morning, me to Hebrew class, and the pigs to market.

The one relaxation which the sisters allowed themselves, apart from church, was knitting, and at about nine in the evening they would switch on the news, open their knitting bags and sit back with needles clicking, emitting an occasional tut at this or that news item. There was no electricity in the house and they worked by gas-light, which they kept turned down low. Arthur, who would come in to hear the news, usually fell asleep as soon as he sat down. The room, for all its size, was always cosy and warm, and sitting among them last thing at night with my mug of cocoa in hand, munching a digestive biscuit, listening to the news, in the soft, greenish flickering light, I felt strangely at one with them. Glasgow, parents, Jews, synagogue, seemed very far away.

The makings of an Englishman

Apart from the black-outs I was barely aware of the war in Annan, and in any case, one did not expect a town of that size to be lit up: bright lights one associated with a metropolis like Glasgow. I had heard an air-raid siren but once, and that on the first afternoon of the war, when German bombers came near the

Forth Bridge, but when I returned to Glasgow towards the end of December, the city seemed to be blacked-out even during the day. I had returned reluctantly in a mood to detest it, and detest it I did.

This was the period of the 'phoney war'. There was no fighting and hardly any bombing, and evacuees were beginning to filter back to town, but no acquaintance of mine was among them ... Father would interrupt his endless, multilingual search for news bulletins to give me an hour or two of private tuition every day. Uncle would also pull me aside on more occasions than I thought necessary to test my Jewish knowledge and was sufficiently impressed to suggest that one day I might be a rabbi. My parents, however, had higher hopes for me by then, and the word 'doctor' was whispered around the house. I felt that loneliness which the only child must feel, except that even only children could expect to find company in the street. I found none. Instead I found company in comics.

... I was eight when I came to Scotland and was now nearly eleven, yet, except for exigencies arising out of the war, I had never been admitted to a non-Jewish home. I made friends in the neighbourhood almost as soon as we moved into Battlefield Gardens, even before I could speak English, though it did not take me long to make myself understood, for small children pick up a language as naturally and as casually as they pick up chicken-pox. We played in the central plot of garden, in the street and on the back-greens. We went to the pictures and football matches together, and played football in the recreation ground over the road from Queens Park. And on sunny days, we took sandwiches and bottles of Barr's Iron Brew and had day-long picnics in the park itself, yet they never invited me back to their homes and I never invited them back to mine. It never occurred to me that they should, for if *goyim* were friendly I did not expect them to be that friendly.

There were twelve households in the four-storey block of flats where we lived, of which two were Jewish; ours on the first floor being one and the family Markson on the top floor the other. We and the Marksons were in and out of each other's homes, but in the twenty years I lived in Glasgow there were only two occasions when I set foot in any of the others. The first was during an air-raid when Father was away from home and

Mother in a desperate moment of insecurity, took us to a down-stairs neighbour, to sit the raid out (nobody in the block ever used the air-raid shelter). The other was, many years later, when a man living above us fell down the stairs and I helped him back up to his flat and his bed. But otherwise I never stepped across a single threshold. Yet this was not due to any hostility or ill-feel-ing. On the contrary we were on the best and most neighbourly terms, but the neighbourliness stopped short at the front door.

I suppose my parents may initially have thought that this was due to anti-Semitism, but it soon became clear that Scottish mid-dle-class homes were castles with the portcullis down and the drawbridge up, for even exchanges between non-Jewish neigh-bours took place in the street, or on the landings, or by the open door, but rarely beyond. Working-class homes, I discovered, were quite different.

In Barovke and Breslev we had lived in open homes with open doors. In time we adapted ourselves to the Scottish closed door, though if I never brought anyone home during our first years in Glasgow it was because I came to realize our home was something less than a palace. There were six of us in the family and a lodger to share three rooms and kitchen, and there were beds everywhere. And more irksome than the beds was the laundry.

When we first came to Glasgow Father was earning £4 15s a week, part of which he sent to relatives in Latvia (we were now *die reiche kreivim* [rich relatives]). Mother could not afford to send laundry out (she may for all I know have taken laundry in) and washed everything by hand, including the bed-linen, in the bath (sometimes together with the smaller children). It must have been a back-breaking job for she had to do it crouching, or on her knees. She had never been so industrious in Barovke where our circumstances were infinitely worse, but in Barovke she was the wife of a public figure and had appearances to keep up; whereas in Glasgow she enjoyed comparative – indeed, complete – anonymity. The difficulty, as far as I was concerned, however, was not the washing, but the drying. In Glasgow there was only the small back-green, which was meant to accommo-date the laundry of a dozen households, and on dry days there would be a rush of housewives with dripping laundry, anxious to stake a place on the line. But it usually rained, if not in the morning, then by the end of the day, and Mother finally forsook the line and dried the laundry on twin poles suspended from the kitchen ceiling, and it hung there day and night like a bleeding Sword of Damocles. Mother put out newspapers to catch the drips, which made things even worse, as we lived in a ceaseless suspension of carbolic and moisture and the slow rat-tat of water on paper. On Thursday night Mother fried her fish, and as the oil vapour rose upwards it met the water vapour coming downwards to form an almost impenetrable fog.

The laundry was only removed from the pole on Friday afternoons in honour of the Sabbath, and if there be any who are disgruntled with life, let them suspend dripping laundry from their ceiling for six days of the week and remove it on the seventh. They will then discover the true nature of happiness.

... Queens Park, the local grammar school, was reopened in September 1942. I had sat the necessary qualifying exam before that in Castle Douglas and got a place. I ... was taken to Paisley's, one of the posher gentlemen's outfitters in town – the sort of place where no regular customer paid cash – and there equipped with a green and gold school tie and school scarf, and socks with green and gold rings at the top and little green tabs for the garters. My parents must have found it all ruinously expensive, but they got more than their money's worth in *naches* [pride].Clad in my new livery, I was paraded round the family, and Liebe Sheine blinked when she saw me: 'Look at him, an Engils gentleman.'

Part 3

FROM THE CENTRAL OFFICE
FOR REFUGEES

Do's and Don't's for Refugees

DO talk English as much as you possibly can. Bad English is preferable to German. The average person does not know what nationality you are by your English accent.

DO make appointments if you have to see any member of the Committees, otherwise you may be kept waiting for a long time and greatly inconvenience other people.

DO obey police regulations and all instructions given to you by officials of the Committees. It is in your own interest.

DO make sure that no lights show anywhere outside your house from sunset to sunrise.

DO be as quiet and modest as possible. If you do not make yourself noticeable other people will not bother about you.

DO be as cheerful as possible. Everyone sympathizes with you in your difficult position. A smiling face makes them still more your friends.

DON'T talk German in the streets, in public places or any place where others may hear you. You will learn English more quickly by talking it constantly. And there is nothing to show the man in the street that you are a Refugee and not a Nazi.

DON'T go to any of the Committees unless you have a definite reason for doing so. They have a great deal to do and callers only hinder their work.

DON'T listen to the thousand and one rumours which fly about. The only authentic information is given over the wireless and in the newspapers.

DON'T join groups or crowds of people in the streets and elsewhere. Crowds cause panic in Air Raids.

DON'T telephone asking for your passports. If they are with one of the Committees they will be returned to you as quickly as possible. If they are with the Home Office the same thing applies.

DON'T ask if your friends and relatives can be brought into the country whether or not they have permits. No one can at present immigrate to this country.

DON'T telephone saying your letter has not been answered. It will be answered as soon as possible.

DON'T go outside a radius of five miles from your home without a Police permit. It is against the law for you to do so and any breach can be severely punished.

DON'T discuss the political situation in public.

Entertaining our Refugee Guests

In a recent address to a group of German refugees and their English friends, the Bishop of Chichester referred to the refugees as 'the reconcilers, the ambassadors of unity, the mediators between nations'. The fact that we have some 65,000 of these victims of Nazi oppression here in Great Britain therefore constitutes an excellent opportunity, not merely for rendering that kind of practical service to some one in need which it is always an Englishman's pleasure to give, but also for keeping alive that spirit of friendship and goodwill between the peoples of different nations apart from which there can be very little hope for the future well-being of mankind as a whole.

The great majority of these refugees came to this country with the reasonable expectation of being able to re-emigrate within a fairly short time of their arrival. The outbreak of war, however, greatly reduced the prospects of such re-emigration and our temporary visitors have no alternative but to remain as permanent guests, at least for the duration of the war. We must, therefore, do our best to help to make them feel at home amongst us.

It is obvious that many of them will have various needs which we must try to meet. The Government has realized the seriousness of their financial plight, and has pledged itself to help the refugee organizations to maintain them. Various social service organizations are doing their best to help with some of their more difficult problems, giving them advice on such matters as employment, insurance, housing and medical and dental facilities. By far the greatest need, however, is for the cooperation of men and women of goodwill in all parts of the country in establishing friendly contact with the refugees. To be a stranger in a strange land, to have very little opportunity of getting to understand its language, its customs and above all, its people – this surely is the worst possible fate that can overtake anyone, and it is from this that we are so anxious to deliver these refugee guests of ours.

In this adventure of friendship all of us can play a part, though it is not always easy for everyone to see just where he fits into the general scheme of things. The following suggestions, which we hope will afford some guidance to those who want to help but do not quite know how to set about it, are all based on reports which have reached us of work that is being done on a small scale in a few places. We should like to see such work springing up wherever there are any refugees living.

1. **SOCIAL CENTRES.** It is an excellent thing to have a recognized hall or house to which refugees can come at stated times, not only to meet each other, but to get into contact with English people. The organization of such centres is exactly the kind of job in which youth groups, clubs, guilds, and the local branches of such movements as YMCA,[1] YWCA,[2] Toc H,[3] and Rotary,[4] and many others can lend a hand. Such centres offer all kinds of interesting possibilities ... English classes for Germans, German classes for English folk, reading circles, musical circles and general discussion groups. The English genius of providing odd cups of tea at all hours of the day and night would probably add quite a good deal to the friendliness of such centres. It might even be possible in some cases to arrange for these light refreshments to be provided free of charge! It should be noted, however, that refugees, like the rest of us, dislike what is commonly called 'charity'. If and when they are able to contribute, they should be given the opportunity to do so. It will help them to maintain their self-respect. An essential function of such centres, of course, is to bring individual refugees into close contact with individual English families, so that from the social centre we work out to:

---

1. Young Men's Christian Association.
2. Young Women's Christian Association.
3. Toc H, Talbot House, founded after the First World War by the Reverend 'Tubby' Clayton.
4. The Rotary Club is an organization of professional and businessmen involved in local charitable work.

2. PRIVATE HOSPITALITY. This may be of several kinds, rang-ing from the evening at home to the weekend or even longer period. The privilege of entertaining refugees in this way is, of course, by no means limited to those who come into contact with them through the social centres referred to above. There are families living in the country who could render most valu-able service by offering a week's or a fortnight's holiday to some refugee who has been having a particularly difficult time under not very cheering conditions in one or other of our large cities.

3. RELIGIOUS SERVICES. Some refugees, for very obvious rea-sons, greatly welcome an opportunity of attending a service conducted in German, and in some places, arrangements have already been made for special services to be held at regular intervals. Many church halls have been lent both to Christian and Jewish refugees, for special services. There is a great deal to be said, too, for holding services partly in English and partly in German to which English people as well as refugees may be invited.

4. ENTERTAINMENTS. Now that we have begun to get used to the black-out, entertainments are coming to have a much more prominent place in our social life. But entertainments usually mean a certain amount of expense, and with the very limited financial resources which most refugees have at their disposal, it is very difficult for them to get to concerts, theatres, etc. This is all the greater a hardship for many of them because in Germany music had played a very important part in their whole life. Here then is a service which organizers of concerts, cinemas and the-atre proprietors can render in making available a number of tick-ets for distribution to people who would tremendously appreci-ate having them.

But since a good deal of the fun in life consists of making one's own amusement, there is plenty of scope for groups of English people and refugees to provide their own programmes for the entertainment of their friends. In this way many compe-tent artists, who are otherwise deprived of any opportunity of practising their art, can be given an opportunity of making a very effective contribution to the general cultural life of the English community as well as their own.

5. **EDUCATIONAL WORK.** We have already referred to English classes in connection with the social centres, but there are other ways of an educational character in which most valuable help can be given to refugees. Many of them, for instance, would greatly appreciate the opportunity of attending lectures on English life, or on the general background of English political, social and cultural life. A vast number require quite elementary information such as the procedure necessary to join a public library, while others can be greatly helped by being introduced to existing organizations which are responsible for day or evening classes.

Many of them would also appreciate opportunities of training in various handicrafts. For those who are just beginning, elementary classes can be arranged, and for those who are already skilled workers, groups can be arranged where articles can be made for sale to shops, and through other channels on a co-operative basis. In this connection it should be noted that application must be made to the Home Office for permission to start such a group, but this permission is as a rule very readily given.

6. **WORKING PARTIES FOR PROVIDING WAR COMFORTS.** Many refugees greatly value the opportunity of making 'comforts' for the Forces as an opportunity of expressing their appreciation of the hospitality which they are enjoying in this country. But since few of them are in a position to provide their own material there is again scope for friendly co-operation between the guest and the host whose privilege it is to provide materials and possibly accommodation for such parties to meet in.

7. **ETCETERAS.** By this time, no doubt, you will have begun to think of all sorts of other ways in which you yourself or the organization or church or synagogue with which you are connected could help. There are rambles to be arranged during the summer, older folk who can be visited in their homes. There is clothing to be provided for folk whose resources do not permit the renewal of their wardrobes and a whole host of other useful bits of services which you will doubtless discover for yourself.

There are only two other things which need be mentioned in conclusion. In the first place, it may well be that while a number of these suggestions appeal to you, you may be rather at a loss to know how to get into touch with the refugees themselves. May we suggest therefore that you approach any local refugee committee in your area or the nearest Citizens' Advice Bureau, or failing that, that you write direct to us:

Welfare Department,
Central Office for Refugees,
Bloomsbury House,
Bloomsbury Street,
London, WC1

It is most likely that the information you require will be readily to hand in your own district, but if it is not, do not hesitate to write to us about any matters relating to the general welfare of refugees.

Secondly, may we stress once more the point made earlier in this leaflet, namely, the fact that it is absolutely vital that in all this work we should regard ourselves not as conferring favours on those, who through no fault of their own, have been placed in the most embarrassing of all circumstances, but rather as fellow-workers with them in promoting the kind of fellowship for one to which the world is in such sorrow [*sic*] plight today.

Mistress and Maid

*General Information for the Use of Domestic Refugees
and their Employers*

THE LEGAL POSITION AND HOUSEHOLD CUSTOMS

EMPLOYMENT. Permission must be obtained by the *mistress* from her local Ministry of Labour Employment Exchange to employ a refugee placed in Class 'C' by the Tribunal. The name of a specific refugee must be given when making the application.

Permission must be obtained from the Home Office before any refugee placed in Class 'B' by the Tribunal may be employed. The Domestic Bureau or the Local Committee are prepared to act on behalf of the employer.

Under no circumstances may any domestic refugee proceed to her new post before such permission is granted, either by the local Employment Exchange or by the Home Office.

WAGES. The wages must be approved by the Employment Exchange or the Home Office, whichever the case may be. Wages and other conditions of service must be equal to those enjoyed by British subjects of the same age in the district for similar work.

BREAKAGES. Breakages cannot be deducted from wages, even where gross negligence can be proved, but if the maid offers to pay for breakage and requests the employer to deduct it from her wages, then the employer is entitled to deduct it, but it is proper for the employer to pay the wages in full and for the servant to tender the amount for breakage.

NOTICE. In the absence of agreement to the contrary, notice is entirely governed by payment of wages. If the wages are paid monthly, then either party can determine the employment at any time on giving one month's notice. If the servant is paid weekly, the notice must be given on the date on which payment is made.

If any particular period of notice has been agreed upon, that notice must be given.

If a maid leaves without giving notice, she forfeits her wages from the last date of payment. She is also liable to be sued for damages caused to her employer by her departure.

A maid is justified in leaving without notice, if she has reasonable cause to fear violence to the person or disease. In such cases the maid is entitled to wages up to the time of leaving.

If the employer requests the maid to leave when a notice (given by either party) has not yet expired, then full wages must be paid up to the date when the notice would expire. This does not apply in cases of wilful disobedience or other misconduct by the maid.

If the employer dismisses the maid instantly, without giving notice, the employer is bound to pay a month's or a week's full wages (according to what the proper notice would be). This does not apply in the case of misconduct, or where the employer has a right to dismiss her without notice.

It is illegal to retain the maid's luggage in any circumstances.

NATIONAL HEALTH INSURANCE. All refugee domestics between the ages of 14 and 65 must be insured and the *employer* is responsible for seeing that this is carried out. For girls under 16 years, 4d is payable by the girl and 4d by the employer. Over 16 years, 7d is paid by the girl and 7d by the employer.

A health insurance card and information regarding Approved Societies and local Panel doctors can be obtained from the nearest Post Office. The maid should immediately join an Approved Society and register with a Panel doctor locally. The card is the property of the maid.

Twenty-six stamps are needed in order to claim Sickness Benefit. If, however, a doctor is required, one can be obtained immediately, as a person becomes entitled to Medical Benefit as soon as he or she insures under the Act. Such benefit does not include hospital treatment. Sickness Benefit is as follows:

Men
26 Contributions and under 104 ... 9s 0d weekly
104   "   and over ... 15s 0d   "

Women
26 Contributions and under 104 ... 7s 6d   "
104   "   and over ... 10s 0d   "

The above is the statutory minimum. By belonging to an Approved Society additional help might be given, according to the rules of the Society.

ILLNESS. The employer is not justified in discharging the maid without notice if she is temporarily ill, and is bound to supply her with food and lodging in addition to wages so long as she continues in the employer's service. The maid's Panel doctor should be called in.

The employer is entitled to discharge the maid without notice in the case of permanent illness or disablement, but full wages must be paid up to the time of her illness.

An employee can claim compensation for injury due to the accident if the accident arises out of or in the course of her employment, unless there is common employment, i.e., where the servant is injured by another servant employed by the same master carrying out the master's instructions or some responsible person placed in authority by the employer.

In cases of long illness or disablement, if the maid's insurance is insufficient, or the employer is unable to provide for her, enquiries may be addressed to the Domestic Bureau.

UNIFORM. It is customary for the maid to wear a cotton uniform in the morning and a dark uniform in the afternoon and evening, together with appropriate caps and aprons. Some employers permit the wearing of overalls. The uniform is bought by the maid and is her property. If the mistress supplies any part of the uniform, those articles should be returned to her when the maid leaves.

SPECIAL POINTS FOR MISTRESSES

Although most refugee domestics have, by now, had some experience in English households, the customs of various houses vary, and to avoid misunderstanding, it is advisable to explain your particular requirements at greater length than would be necessary with an English maid.

* * *

Many of these girls are trying to forget their terrible experiences before they found shelter in this country. They dread loneliness, and therefore settle down much better and work more efficiently if the mistress encourages them to make friends in their spare time, etc., as suggested in the section entitled 'Social and Educational Opportunities'.

* * *

We shall be pleased to forward to mistresses who are interested in the welfare of their domestics during their free time, a booklet entitled 'Entertaining Our Refugee Guests', written by the Welfare Department, which gives further details of the girls' backgrounds and of the opportunities which may be afforded to them to assist in the process of 'acclimatization'.

SPECIAL POINTS FOR MAIDS

POLICE REGULATIONS. Be careful to carry out fully all Police Regulations in regard to notifying change of address, etc. You cannot be too scrupulous in these matters.

WARNING. Do remember that it will cause very grave trouble if you attempt to get in touch with relatives and friends in Germany (even through friends in neutral countries) unless you do so in the authorized manner – through the British Red Cross. Any Citizen's Advice Bureau will give you particulars.

IT IS ILLEGAL to send money, even through neutral countries, to relatives in Germany. Moreover, the money would probably never reach them.

RATION CARDS. Read the instructions carefully on your ration cards. If you go to a new post, hand over your book to your mistress, having first carried out the necessary formalities for change of residence. If you leave a post, remember to ask for the return of your ration book and see that you have the proper numbers of coupons left, otherwise these must be returned to you.

MEDICAL HELP. Do not incur expenses for dental and optical work for which you cannot pay. For any attention not covered by your Health Insurance, you should write to the Domestic Bureau, who will arrange for you to receive treatment. The Bureau does not pay accounts which it has not authorized.

LUGGAGE. The Domestic Bureau cannot be responsible for any luggage. You should write to the Domestic Bureau at Bloomsbury House and ask for advice before storing or sending your luggage to any given place, other than an employer's house.

SAVINGS. Open a Post Office Savings Bank Account at once. Interest is given and sums up to £3 can be withdrawn on demand. It is important that you should have some money put aside for holidays, illness and to support you if you are out of work. The Domestic Bureau will not be able to give you unlimited assistance.

You can also put your money into National Savings, and should enquire at the local Post Office for the address of the Secretary of a National Savings Society.

UNEMPLOYMENT. If you are out of work, you should register immediately with the local Ministry of Labour Employment Exchange for work, and report there once a week until you have found a post. You can also register with private Employment Agencies and should advise your local committee, or the Domestic Bureau that you are in need of work.

HOLIDAYS. The Domestic Bureau will be pleased to send particulars of accommodation in pleasant country and seaside surroundings at 25s per week for girls desiring to take a holiday.

ENGLISH MANNERS AND CUSTOMS. In this country it is good manners to speak and walk quietly, both in the house and in the street and public places. You will notice that the mistress usually states her requirements in the form of a request. This should be carried out at once as an order. It is not correct to argue with a mistress.

Do not grumble because English household customs are different from Continental ones. Adapt yourself as quickly as possible to your new surroundings. English houses are often colder than Continental ones, and you must expect to guard against the cold by wearing thick underclothes and woollen indoor coats.

LANGUAGE. Do your best to improve your knowledge of English, and **always speak English in the streets and public places**. Read English books and newspapers and learn as much as you can about English history and literature, so that you may understand English ways of living and thinking.

SOCIAL AND EDUCATIONAL OPPORTUNITIES. You need not be lonely. The Domestic Bureau will be glad to put you in touch with (1) other girls and English families in the neighbourhood; (2) local social clubs and institutions; or (3) social workers or educational bodies who will supply you with lists of classes and lecturers, or concerts, which you may like to attend in your free time. Books may be borrowed free of charge from any Public Library (often situated near the local Town Hall).

KEEP IN TOUCH WITH THE BUREAU. The best way of securing the full help of the Domestic Bureau is to keep in touch with it regularly. Please send a postcard each month, giving your christian and surname, your permit or yellow card number. All you need say is: 'This is to advise you that I am still at the above address.' Change of address should also be advised immediately, both to the Bureau and to your local committee.

IN CASE OF DIFFICULTIES. If you cannot get in touch with the Domestic Bureau or your local committee, turn at once to the police, who are always most kind and helpful to those in trouble.

April 1940

DOMESTIC BUREAU

Central Office for Refugees,
Bloomsbury House,
Bloomsbury Street,
London, WC1

Licensed by the LCC
Phone: MUSeum 2900

DEPOTS

35 Shoot Up Hill, London, NW2

Phone: GLAdstone 6296

Toynbee Hall, Commercial Street, London, E1

Phone: BIShopsgate 6467

38 Fitzroy Square, London, WC1

Phone: MUSeum 4358

6 Queen's Gardens, London, W2

Phone: PADdington 0306

NOTE:

Domestics in the London Metropolitan area should call at their nearest depot for any guidance or information required. The Yellow Domestic Registration Card must be produced at each visit. If a domestic does not hold such a card, she should call and register at Bloomsbury House before going to her Depot.

Domestics in country districts should write to Bloomsbury House for information regarding their nearest Provincial Committee, etc.